I0467643

My Life as a Pro Se Plaintiff

REPRESENTING MYSELF IN COURT

CYNTHIA FISHER

I am dedicating this
book to the Lord Jesus
Christ. He always has
my back.

Table of Contents

Introduction

My Life as a Pro Se Plaintiff

Introduction

Hello, my name is Cynthia Ann Fisher. However, I am known as Cindy. I have a Doctorate of Pharmacy degree and an Executive Juris Doctor degree. I am not a licensed attorney yet but I hope to be. Granted I probably know more than the average person concerning the law. However, the procedures and paper work are definitely trial and error for me. I used the IRAC format for each complaint. I learned this in law school. I = Issue; R = Rule; A = Analysis; C = Conclusion.

I am writing this book to give as much help as I can to people who find themselves in situations when someone or a company has hurt you both civilly and criminally. I have experienced both. And the cases I am going to describe really happened. I will be using real names and places. I will also be sharing the evidence I have for each case. I am protected by the first amendment of the Constitution and have the right to tell my story or should I say present my case to the public.

A person that is Pro Se is defending herself in court. Also, remember that ignorance of the law is no excuse, especially under tort law. Keep in mind, that when you fight you need to be fighting for the Lord. We work for the Lord and not ourselves. Have faith in the Lord. I prayed before each and every legal action I have taken. I needed the Lord to guide me because I was definitely working outside my comfort zone.

The following are the civil complaints I have filed Pro Se:
Cynthia Fisher vs. Carl Whaley, John Whaley, Choice Med, Inc..., and Alliance Bank &Trust
Cynthia Fisher vs. Community Pharmacy
Cynthia Fisher vs. Thomas Norkus, Emily Williams, David Williams, and William Joe Goodman

There are both civil and criminal issues in all of these. I have filed a criminal complaint or complaints against Carl, Whaley, John Whaley, Harriet Whaley, Shelia Cooper, Alliance Bank & Trust, and Community Pharmacy. The criminal investigation has begun. However, I did try everything thru the civil legal process before having to initiate criminal complaints.

Some of the complaints or accusations I have described in this book is my opinion or comes under the term alleged because the criminal accusations have not been proven in a court of law yet. In my opinion, I was forced into bankruptcy because of the criminal and unlawful civil behavior that the Whaleys, Alliance Bank & Trust, and Community Pharmacy participated in. Everything described in this book, is now part of the public record of the NC Court System. All civil and criminal complaints have been given to the police and District Attorneys of Cleveland and Mecklenburg Counties. As far as I know, the District Attorney of Cleveland County has started their investigations. I do not know about the District Attorney of Mecklenburg County. I do hope so.

I.   Carl Whaley, John Whaley, and Med Choice Inc.

The first civil complaint I filed as a Pro Se plaintiff was 13-CVS-579. The lawsuit was against John Whaley, Carl Whaley, Choice Med Inc., and Alliance Bank & Trust. I did have a licensed attorney at first. Her name is Maggie Jaynes. She eventually became my legal coach because I ran out of money and had to file the complaint Pro Se. This is how my first complaint was both pro se and using an attorney.

John and Carl Whaley did a countersuit against me. I finally had to declare bankruptcy and let the bankruptcy trustee settle it because I was totally out of money. However, the bankruptcy trustee did settle out of court with John and Carl Whaley and Med Choice Inc. using my Pro Se complaint.

John and Carl Whaley had a legal purchase/sell agreement to purchase fifty percent of Fisher Rx Direct. There is a copy of this contract in the appendix. There is a copy of the buy/sell contract in which John and Carl Whaley tried to coerce me into signing. I did not sign it because my attorney told me not and it did not look right to me. It was an illegal contract because it rewrote the original contract to purchase fifty percent of Fisher Rx Direct. A contract with the purpose to get the party to break a legally binding contract that the party has already made is an illegal contract. That is what Carl and John Whaley tried to get me to do.

A. Conversion

Issue: Tort of Conversion

Rule: The tort of conversion occurs when the defendant so substantially interferes with the plaintiff's possession or ownership of property that it is fair to require the defendant to pay the property's full value. See Rest. 2d §222A. It is irrelevant that the defendant did not know that the action would constitute a tort or a crime. Thus in the law of intentional torts, "ignorance of the law is no excuse."

The intentional tortfeasor will be liable for virtually every result stemming directly or even somewhat indirectly from his conduct, however unlikely it might have seemed at the time of his act that this result would follow. Rest. 2d, §435B.

Analysis: I was 50 percent owner of Fisher Rx Direct and Whaley Communications is 50 percent owner of Fisher Rx Direct. Carl Whaley and John Whaley are head of Whaley Communications. Carl and John Whaley sold the patient files and other assets of Fisher Rx Direct to Community Pharmacy (Shelby Family Pharmacy). I was willing to continue to be a partner of workout a fair buyback agreement. However, John and Carl Whaley did not want to do that. The Whaleys (Whaley Communications) had already sold the patient files of Fisher Rx Direct to Community Pharmacy, without her knowledge or consent, while trying to coerce Ms. Fisher into signing an agreement that was horrible and could have destroyed her. The harm done to Fisher Rx Direct was its complete destruction. The expense and inconvenience caused to Ms. Fisher was considerable. Carl and John Whaley had illegally taken my name off of the Fisher Rx Direct Bank account at Alliance Bank. John Whaley is on the Board of Directors of Alliance Bank. Carl and John Whaley have refused to let me have access to the Fisher Rx Direct account at Alliance Bank for several months and continued to do so. Ms. Marquez, my attorney, had contacted Mr. Farmer, the attorney for Carl Whaley, John Whaley, and Med. Choice Inc., on several occasions concerning all these matters. The amount that Fisher Rx Direct received from Community Pharmacy for patient files and other assets is still in question, because that information has never been given to me. Carl and John Whaley refused to pay for Ms. Fisher's attorney even after they were told that Fisher Rx Direct had to pay for my attorney, and they refused to pay checks written on the Fisher Rx Direct account, even after they were told they had to. The checks written by me for monthly expenses for me never exceeded what I was owed in salary. Carl and John Whaley had Alliance Bank & Trust bounce any checks I wrote on the business account, even after being told I had the legal right to write those checks. I was trying to survive while I legally tried to take back my pharmacy. The Whaleys tried to make sure I could not legally do anything to them because they forced me into bankruptcy. They did not count on the Lord backing me. The Lord continues to bless me because I work for him now instead of myself.

Conclusion: The Whaleys have no defenses because of what they tried to do to me. Carl Whaley and John Whaley sold patient files and closed Fisher Rx Direct without my knowledge or consent. John and Carl Whaley owe me compensation for the conversion of my half of Fisher Rx Direct. I had no choice but to get control of some funds of Fisher Rx Direct in order to pay my attorney and pay my bills. Mr. Carl and John Whaley tried to bankrupt me, so she could not take them to court. Mr. Carl and John Whaley opened a new account for Fisher Rx Direct at Alliance Bank & Trust and shut down the old account for Fisher Rx Direct at Alliance Bank & Trust. The actions I had to take is considered self-defense because John and Carl Whaley stole my fifty percent of Fisher Rx Direct. John and Carl Whaley only owned fifty percent of Fisher Rx Direct and not 100 percent. John and Carl Whaley embezzled over a $100,000 from Fisher Rx Direct because when they sold the patient files and other assets of Fisher Rx Direct, they pocketed 100 percent of the proceeds from the sale. I have not been told how much the patient files or other assets of Fisher Rx Direct were sold for. When John and Carl Whaley sold my fifty percent of patient files and other assets of Fisher Rx Direct, they commented larceny. John and Carl

Whaley committed embezzlement when they pocketed the money from the sell concerning my fifty percent of patient files and other assets of Fisher Rx Direct. John and Carl Whaley did not own 100 percent of Fisher Rx Direct patient files and other assets, they only owned fifty percent.

B. Interference with Existing Contracts

Issue: Interference with existing contracts

It is irrelevant that the defendant did not know that the action would constitute a tort or a crime. Thus in the law of intentional torts, "ignorance of the law is no excuse." The intentional tortfeasor will be liable for virtually every result stemming directly or even somewhat indirectly from his conduct, however unlikely it might have seemed at the time of his act that this result would follow. Rest. 2d, §435B.

Rule: The plaintiff loses the benefits of existing contracts.

Analysis: A prima facie case exists for the tort of interference with existing contracts occur when the plaintiff loses the benefits of existing contracts. The selling of the patient files and other assets of Fisher Rx Direct was interference with existing contracts. The pharmacy lost several patients because I was not allowed back into her pharmacy. The patients stated they would come back when I came back. Furthermore, Fisher Rx Direct was a back-up pharmacy for Hospice, as well as several nursing homes and assisted living centers. Fisher Rx Direct lost these contracts when Carl and John Whaley destroyed Fisher Rx Direct.

Conclusion: Whaley Communications owes me compensatory damages for interference with existing contracts. This occurred because John and Carl Whaley stole my fifty percent of patient files and other assets of Fisher Rx Direct.

C. Interference with Prospective Advantage

Issue: Interference with Prospective Advantage

Rule: The plaintiff loses the benefits of prospective contracts

Analysis: A prima facie case exists for the tort of interference of prospective contracts occur when the plaintiff loses not the benefits of an existing contract, but simply the benefits of prospective, potential contracts or other relationships. The destruction of Fisher Rx Direct interfered with the benefits of prospective, potential contracts or other relationships. I had been getting more customers for the business while I was trying to get control back of Fisher Rx Direct. Also, I was hoping to work out something with the City of Shelby when I found out they needed a pharmacy to work with them, so the city employees would be able to afford their medication. The City of Shelby needs a good prescription plan.

Conclusion: Carl and John Whaley owes me compensation when they illegally took control of Fisher Rx Direct away from me for the benefit of prospective, potential contracts.

D. Malicious Prosecution

Issue: Malicious Prosecution
Rule: To make out a prima facie case of malicious prosecution, the plaintiff must prove the following elements: (1) that the defendant instituted criminal proceedings against him; (2) that these proceedings terminated in favor of the plaintiff (the accused); (3) that the defendant had no probable cause to institute the proceedings; and (4) that the defendant was motivated primarily by some purpose other than bringing an offender to justice. See Rest. 2d, §653; P&K, p. 871.

Initiating proceeding: The plaintiff must show that the defendant took an active part in instigating and encouraging the prosecution. For instance, if the defendant merely states what she believes to be the facts to the prosecutor, and leaves to the latter the decision whether to prosecute, this will probably not be "institution" of proceedings. But if the defendant has attempted to influence a district attorney to prosecute, or has lied so as to make prosecution more probable, this will be sufficient. See P&K, p. 872-73.

i.   Mistake of law: But a lay person's erroneous belief that certain conduct constitutes a crime is quite likely to be held to be unreasonable, if it is not arrived at after consultation with a lawyer or prosecutor. Once the defendant does receive assurances of her lawyer or the prosecutor that these facts constitute a crime, however, she has probable cause (assuming that she has made full disclosure of the facts known to her). See Rest. 2d, §662, Comment i and §666.

ii.   The intentional tortfeasor will be liable for virtually every result stemming directly or even somewhat indirectly from his conduct, however unlikely it might have seemed at the time of his act that this result would follow. Rest. 2d, §435B.

Analysis: From what I understand John Whaley lied to the DA to try and have me prosecuted for forgery and/or fraud. He told the DA that I had no legal right to write checks on the Fisher Rx Direct business account because he had fired me. Neither John Whaley nor Carl Whaley had to legal right to fire me because I was 50% owner of Fisher Rx Direct. I did fire an employee for directly disobeying a direct order from me and I had the legal right to do that as 50% owner of Fisher Rx Direct. Carl Whaley admitted to the detective that came to my house that I was 50% owner of Fisher Rx Direct. I provided proof of 50% ownership to the detective and the warrant was dismissed by the DA. I believe that Mr. John Whaley's actions were pure vindictiveness because I would not let him have total control of Fisher Rx Direct. I was willing to still be partner or work out a fair buyout agreement, in which case I could buy them out. Mr. John Whaley was not willing to do this. Mr. Carl Whaley might have felt the same way but I do not think so, because he had told me himself personally he did not enjoy working in the pharmacy, he preferred working outside. I do not think that neither Carl nor John Whaley consulted their attorney or the DA before sending back checks from the Fisher Rx Direct Alliance Bank Account accusing me of forgery/fraud. I believe this because the checks were sent back after they cleared the bank. The checks I wrote against the Alliance bank account were for bills and attorney fees and I was being refused my salary by Carl and John Whaley. They were trying to bankrupt me in order to take my business, so I could not hire an attorney. The DA stopped the proceedings as soon as I proved that I was 50% owner of Fisher Rx Direct. According to the contract between Whaley Communications and Fisher Rx Direct (Dr. Cynthia A. Fisher), all attorney fees for each party are to be paid for by Fisher Rx Direct.

Conclusion: I have an action against Med Inc., John and Carl Whaley for lost income which comes under compensatory damages, and punitive damages for intentional infliction of emotional and mental distress.

E. Defamation of Character

Issue: Defamation of Character

Rule: To be defamatory, a statement must have a tendency to harm the reputation of the plaintiff. Rest. 2d, §559: For the statement to be defamatory, it is not necessary that it have actually injured the plaintiff's reputation; it must simply be the case that, if it had been believed, it would have had this effect. Thus even if the defendant can show that everyone who heard the statement believed that it was false, this will not prevent the statement from being defamatory. The defamatory statement must have an element of disgrace, the group the statement is communicated to must be respectable, and the statement must have a defamatory meaning. Libel is defamation in written form and slander is defamation in oral form or if there is special harm involved. Cases where no special harm necessary ("slander per se"): There are four kinds of utterances which, even though they are slander rather than libel, require no showing of special harm. These categories derive from a variety of historical factors, but their common element is that they are by their very nature especially likely to cause pecuniary harm. Such slander is generally called "slander per se." See P&K, p. 788-93. The categories are as follows: a.

Crime: Statements imputing criminal behavior to the plaintiff. However, an accusation of a minor crime (e.g., a parking ticket) is not generally enough. The Restatement requires that the conduct imputed to the plaintiff either be "punishable by imprisonment" or "regarded by public opinion as involving moral turpitude". Rest. 2d, §571. The defamatory statement must be seen or heard by someone other than plaintiff.

Ignorance of the law no excuse: Similarly, it is irrelevant that the defendant did not know that the action would constitute a tort or a crime. Thus in the law of intentional torts, "ignorance of the law is no excuse."

The intentional tortfeasor will be liable for virtually every result stemming directly or even somewhat indirectly from his conduct, however unlikely it might have seemed at the time of his act that this result would follow. Rest. 2d, §435B.

Analysis: Carl and John Whaley accused me of forgery and fraud, with actual malice. Actual malice is when the defendant knew statement was false or recklessly disregarded the truth. Both Carl and John Whaley knew what they were accusing me of was false and they did not care about the truth. The conduct imputed to me could have been punishable by imprisonment. Carl and John Whaley told Alliance Bank that the checks I wrote to pay my salary and bills were forgery and fraud even though I had a legal right to write checks on the Fisher Rx Direct bank account at Alliance Bank because I owned 50% of Fisher Rx Direct. The special harm caused to me was that First National Bank closed my personal account because I was accused of forgery and fraud. I also had to pay fees on returned checks which Carl and John Whaley refused to pay even after they were told they had to. Forgery and fraud were written on the returned checks.

Conclusion: Whaley Communications, John, and Carl Whaley owes me compensatory and punitive damages for Defamation of Character because special harm was caused.

F. Coercion

Issue: Coercion

Rule: Coercion is the practice of forcing another party to act in an involuntary manner by use of intimidation or threats or some other form of pressure or force. It involves a set of various types of forceful actions that violate the free will of an individual to induce a desired response, usually having a strict choice or option against a person in such a way a victim cannot escape

Analysis: Carl and John Whaley tried to force me into signing a horrible contract and they would not let me into the Fisher Rx Direct Bank account unless I signed it.

Conclusion: I did not sign the contract and was not allowed to get back into the Fisher Rx Direct bank account. It was attempted coercion but in North Carolina, attempting satisfies the requirement for the crime.

G. Abuse of Process

Issue: Abuse of process

Rule: Abuse of process: Even if a criminal or civil proceeding is brought with probable cause, and for allowable motives, a person involved in it may use various litigation devices available to him during the course of it for improper purposes. If so, he will be liable for "abuse of process."
Ignorance of the law no excuse: Similarly, it is irrelevant that the defendant did not know that the action would constitute a tort or a crime. Thus in the law of intentional torts, "ignorance of the law is no excuse."

The intentional tortfeasor will be liable for virtually every result stemming directly or even somewhat indirectly from his conduct, however unlikely it might have seemed at the time of his act that this result would follow. Rest. 2d, §435B.

Analysis: Mr. Carl Whaley and Mr. John Whaley had Alliance bank send back checks that I wrote to pay bills and my attorney by telling the bank it was forgery/fraud. Mr. John Whaley is on the Board of Directors of Alliance and I believe Mr. John Whaley was able to get this done without going thru proper channels because of his position on the Board of Directors at Alliance Bank & Trust. Alliance refused to allow me access to the Fisher Rx Direct bank account even after being told that I had the legal right to have access to that account. Mr. John Whaley and Mr. Carl Whaley still refused to pay the checks even after they were told that I had the legal right to write checks on the Fisher Rx Direct Alliance bank account. Carl and John Whaley paid for their attorney from the Fisher Rx Direct bank account but refused to pay my attorney from the Fisher Rx Direct bank account.

Conclusion: Mr. John and Mr. Carl Whaley were being vindictive and malicious in their abuse of process. I would like the bank to require that Mr. John Whaley step down from being on the Board of Directors of Alliance bank and should not be allowed to be on the Board of Directors of any bank again. I might have actions against Alliance Bank because they allowed John and Carl Whaley to take me off the bank account without checking with me and I am the only one that should have had the authority to take myself off the of the Fisher Rx Direct Alliance Bank account. The DA has resolved everything in my favor.

H. Intentional Infliction of Emotional Distress

Issue: Intentional Infliction of Mental and Emotional Distress

Rule: Intentional or reckless infliction, by extreme and outrageous conduct, of severe emotional or mental distress, even in the absence of physical harm. Intent: In the intentional torts we have examined so far (battery, assault and false imprisonment), we have seen that the requisite intent may exist not only where the defendant desires to cause a certain result, but also where she knows with "substantial certainty" that the result will occur. In the case of infliction of mental distress, however, the necessary mental state is even broader—there are three possible mental states on D's part, any of which will qualify: [a] D desires to cause P emotional distress; [b] D knows with substantial certainty that P will suffer emotional distress; and [c] D recklessly disregards the high probability that emotional distress will occur.

Ignorance of the law no excuse: Similarly, it is irrelevant that the defendant did not know that the action would constitute a tort or a crime. Thus in the law of intentional torts, "ignorance of the law is no excuse."
Punitive damages: An intentional tort victim may recover punitive damages, if the defendant's conduct was outrageous or malicious. Rest. 2d, §908.

The intentional tortfeasor will be liable for virtually every result stemming directly or even somewhat indirectly from his conduct, however unlikely it might have seemed at the time of his act that this result would follow. Rest. 2d, §435B.

Analysis: Carl and John Whaley of Whaley Communications knew exactly what I had gone thru this past year and they committed all of the torts discussed in this brief anyway. I could not afford insurance because Carl and John Whaley refused to pay me even after they were told I had the legal right to get paid from Fisher Rx Direct. Carl and John Whaley refused to pay Kings Law Offices even after they were told they had to because of the buy/sell agreement between me and Whaley Communications. Carl and John Whaley of Whaley Communications deliberately desired to cause me emotional distress, knew with substantial certainty that I would suffer emotional distress, and recklessly disregarded the high probability that emotional distress would occur. Each and every action of Carl and John Whaley that was committed against me was an intentional tort.

Conclusion: I can collect punitive damages from John and Carl Whaley, and Whaley Communications (Med Choice Inc.) based on the intentional actions of Carl and John Whaley. The actions of Carl and John Whaley were extreme and outrageous and caused severe emotional trauma. An intentional tort victim may recover punitive damages, if the defendant's conduct was outrageous or malicious. Rest. 2d, §908.

I. Misrepresentation

Issue: Intentional Misrepresentation

Rule: A prima facie case of misrepresentation exists when there is a misrepresentation by the defendant. The defendant must have a culpable state of mind, the defendant must have the intent to induce the plaintiff's reliance on the misrepresentation, and cause damage to the plaintiff.

Analysis: Carl Whaley made a misrepresentation to Ms. Fisher, had a culpable state of mind, had the intent to induce Ms. Fisher's reliance on the misrepresentation and caused damage to Ms. Fisher because he sold patient files and closed Fisher Rx Direct. Carl and John Whaley tried to coerce me into signing an unconscionable contract in order to buy back the business. An agreement that is grossly unjust, unfair, or dishonest may be deemed an unconscionable contract. Determining whether or not an agreement is unconscionable usually raises questions of competency, fairness, and honesty. If it is found that these things have been manipulated in such a way that an agreement is shocking to the conscience of a normal person, a court will not allow the contract to be enforced. Ms. Fisher and her attorney, Ms. Marquez have a copy of said contract and will be submitting the contract as evidence against Mr. Carl Whaley, Mr. John Whaley, and Choice Med Inc. The contract will provide proof of the value of the pharmacy. Furthermore, I discovered after talking to honest business people that she is owed further compensation because of putting the funds received from the buy-sell agreement back into the business. Choice Med Inc, Carl Whaley, and John Whaley owe compensation to Fisher Rx Direct because they were supposed to match any funds I put back into the business. Instead of putting the funds from the selling of fifty percent of Fisher Rx Direct into my pocket, I put the funds back into Fisher Rx Direct and Choice Med Inc, Carl Whaley, and John Whaley did not put any more funds into Fisher Rx Direct. The final payment for fifty percent of Fisher Rx Direct was made in January 2010. I later found out that the funds from the buy-sell agreement should have went into my pocket; Carl Whaley, and John Whaley were supposed to put matching funds back into Fisher Rx Direct because they were now fifty percent partners.

Conclusion: Choice Med Inc, Carl Whaley, and John Whaley, owe Ms. Fisher compensation because of the tort of misrepresentation. Carl and John Whaley made a misrepresentation to me, had a culpable state of mind, had the intent to induce Ms. Fisher's reliance on the misrepresentation and caused damage to me because they sold patient files and other assets and closed Fisher Rx Direct. I think the patient files and other assets of Fisher Rx Direct had already been sold when Carl and John Whaley tried to get me to sign the buyout agreement.

II.   <u>Alliance Bank & Trust</u>

I was able to file a default judgment against Alliance Bank and Trust. I was able to file a default judgement because Alliance Bank & Trust did not answer the complaint against them. The bankruptcy trustee gave me back control of the default judgment. However, Alliance Bank & Trust was able to get the default judgment against them dismissed because I did not show up in court. I did not know I was supposed to. Honestly, I was traveling with Walgreens a lot, but I had hired a licensed attorney to handle it for me and he did not. I was able to get my money back from the attorney that did not do his job. So make sure you keep on top of everything and be prepared to go to court yourself. The default judgment against Alliance Bank & Trust was dismissed on September 3, 2014 for the simple reason I was not there. And I did not know I was supposed to be there. Keep on top of court dates and make sure you receive all the notifications concerning court you are supposed to. I think that occurred also. I want to verify that I never had a personal checking account with Alliance Bank & Trust but I did have a business bank account with them thru Fisher Rx Direct. I had to sign signature cards when the Fisher Rx Direct bank account was open. The Fisher Rx Direct business bank account was closed by Carl and John Whaley. I would love to know why my name was taken off the Fisher Rx Direct business bank account by Alliance Bank & Trust. If they had to have me sign a signature card to open the account and I was fifty percent owner of Fisher Rx Direct, I would love to know why I was not informed when the bank took my name off of the Fisher Rx Direct bank account. John nor Carl Whaley had my permission to remove my name from the Fisher Rx Direct business bank account. They could take their names off but not my name off. The default judgment against Alliance Bank & Trust I was dismissed because of my own carelessness. That does not mean, they did not do anything wrong. Kelly Young, the branch manager at Alliance Bank & Trust in Shelby, NC knew everything and knew that I was fifty percent owner of Fisher Rx Direct because I had to prove it when the original Fisher Rx Direct business bank account was opened at Alliance Bank & Trust. The very first business bank account at Fisher Rx Direct was opened at Carolina Bank and TD Bank bought out Carolina Bank. And Carl Whaley and I moved the Fisher Rx Direct to Alliance Bank & Trust at John Whaley's recommendation. In my opinion, Alliance Bank & Trust did not live up to the bank industry standards. I do not ever plan on using Alliance Bank & Trust again for business. And I never used it for my personal banking.

Alliance Bank & Trust is now part of a criminal complaint and I have gone to the banking commission and filed a formal complaint. I did go to the banking commission right after I filed the complaint but they could not get involved because it was in litigation. Now the banking commission can get involved. On October 22, 2015, I sent a complaint to the North Carolina Banking Commission concerning Alliance Bank & Trust and John Whaley. Alliance Bank & Trust has until November 13, 2015 to answer my complaint. Alliance Bank & Trust actions were a major conflict of interest because John Whaley is on the Board of Directors of Alliance Bank & Trust.

A. Conversion

Conversion occurs when the defendant so substantially interferes with plaintiff's possession of ownership of property that it is fair to require the defendant to pay the property's full value. John Whaley was or is on the Board of Directors of Alliance Bank & Trust. Alliance Bank & Trust helped John Whaley take over 100 percent of the Fisher Rx Direct business bank account because of his position on the Board of Directors of Alliance Bank & Trust. Alliance Bank & Trust should have frozen the business bank account of Fisher Rx Direct instead of backing John and Carl Whaley. Alliance Bank & Trust conspired with John and Carl Whaley, so they are accomplices in the crimes of larceny and embezzlement. And of course, they helped Carl and John take 100 percent control of the Fisher Rx Direct business bank account.

B. Interference with Existing Contracts

Alliance Bank & Trust interfered with existing contracts of Fisher Rx Direct because Alliance Bank & Trust conspired with Carl and John Whaley to deprive me of my fifty percent ownership of Fisher Rx Direct. When Alliance Bank & Trust conspired with Carl and John Whaley to deprive me of my fifty ownership in Fisher Rx Direct, because John Whaley was or is on the Board of Directors of Alliance Bank & Trust. Alliance Bank & Trust became accomplices in the larceny and embezzlement scheme of John and Carl Whaley because of their preceding actions.

C. Interference with Prospective Advantage

Alliance Bank & Trust interfered with prospective advantage of Fisher Rx Direct. Prospective advantage deals with the interference of future contracts. Alliance Bank & Trust conspired with Carl and John Whaley to deprive me of my fifty percent ownership of Fisher Rx Direct because John Whaley is on the Board of Directors of Alliance Bank & Trust. The preceding actions of Alliance Bank &

Trust made them accomplices in the larceny and embezzlement scheme of John and Carl Whaley.

D. Defamation of Character

Alliance Bank & Trust committed the tort of defamation of character against me when they sent back checks and wrote forgery and/or fraud on them even though they knew I owned fifty percent of Fisher Rx Direct. For the statement to be defamatory, it is not necessary that it have actually injured the plaintiff's reputation; it must simply be the case that, if it had been believed, it would have had this effect. Thus even if the defendant can show that everyone who heard the statement believed that it was false, this will not prevent the statement from being defamatory. The defamatory statement must have an element of disgrace, the group the statement is communicated to must be respectable, and the statement must have a defamatory meaning. Libel is defamation in written form and slander is defamation in oral form or if there is special harm involved. Cases where no special harm necessary ("slander per se"): There are four kinds of utterances which, even though they are slander rather than libel, require no showing of special harm. These categories derive from a variety of historical factors, but their common element is that they are by their very nature especially likely to cause pecuniary harm. Such slander is generally called "slander per se." See P&K, p. 788-93. The categories are as follows: a. crime: Statements imputing criminal behavior to the plaintiff. However, an accusation of a minor crime (e.g., a parking ticket) is not generally enough. The Restatement requires that the conduct imputed to the plaintiff either be "punishable by imprisonment" or "regarded by public opinion as involving moral turpitude". Rest. 2d, §571. The defamatory statement must be seen or heard by someone other than plaintiff. Ignorance of the law no excuse: Similarly, it is irrelevant that the defendant did not know that the action would constitute a tort or a crime. Thus in the law of intentional torts, "ignorance of the law is no excuse."

The intentional tortfeasor will be liable for virtually every result stemming directly or even somewhat indirectly from his conduct, however unlikely it might have seemed at the time of his act that this result would follow. Rest. 2d, §435B.

The special harm caused to me was that First National Bank closed my personal account because I was accused of forgery and fraud and I could have been imprisoned. Alliance Bank & Trust returned checks to various people and businesses with forgery/fraud written on the returned checks. This means that the defamation was considered libel because it was written. I also had to pay returned check fees. Alliance Bank & Trust owes me compensatory and punitive damages for defamation of character.

E. Abuse of Process

Abuse of process occurs even if a criminal or civil proceeding is brought with probable cause, and for allowable motives, a person involved in it may use various litigation devices available to him during the course of it for improper purposes. If so, he or she will be liable for "abuse of process."

Ignorance of the law no excuse: Similarly, it is irrelevant that the defendant did not know that the action would constitute a tort or a crime. Thus in the law of intentional torts, "ignorance of the law is no excuse." The intentional tortfeasor will be liable for virtually every result stemming directly or even somewhat indirectly from his conduct, however unlikely it might have seemed at the time of his act that this result would follow. Rest. 2d, §435B.

Alliance Bank & Trust refused to honor checks written by me on the Fisher Rx Direct bank account and returned checks after the checks cleared the bank even after they were told they had to honor the checks because I had a right to write checks from the Fisher Rx Direct bank account. Checks were returned after I resubmitted them after the bank was told I had the right to write checks on the

Fisher Rx Direct. The checks that I wrote never exceeded my salary except for attorney fees. Fisher Rx Direct was supposed to pay for both attorney fees, mine and the Whaleys. The Whaleys paid for their attorney from Fisher Rx but refused to pay for mine. Alliance Bank and Trust refused to honor the checks written to my attorney by me from the Fisher Rx Direct business bank account.

F. Negligent Infliction of Emotional Distress

There are 5 components of a prima facie case for negligent infliction of emotional distress and they are: duty, failure to conform, causation in fact, proximate cause, and actual damages. Plaintiff must show that defendant owed plaintiff a legal duty to conduct himself according to certain standards, so as to avoid unreasonable risks to others. Alliance Bank & Trust owed me a duty to be honest and should have checked with me before taking my name off of the Fisher Rx Direct bank account when John and Carl Whaley requested they take my name off of the Fisher Rx Direct business bank account without my permission. Alliance Bank & Trust did not conduct themselves according to the standards of the banking industry in order to avoid unreasonable risk to me. Alliance Bank & Trust failure to conform to industry banking standards is considered lack of reasonable care. The carelessness of Alliance Bank & Trust imposed an unreasonable risk of harm. The failure to conform allowed John and Carl Whaley to force me into bankruptcy and helped John and Carl Whaley embezzle over a 100,000 or more from Fisher Rx Direct. In short, the negligent of Alliance Bank & Trust was cause in fact of my injury. There is a sufficiently close connection or causal link between the negligent act of Alliance Bank & Trust and the injuries caused to me. I suffered actual damages from the negligence of Alliance Bank & Trust. In my opinion, Alliance Bank & Trust were as guilty as John and Carl Whaley because Alliance Bank & Trust sided with John Whaley because he is on the Board of Directors of Alliance Bank & Trust.

G. Coercion

Coercion is the practice of forcing another party to act in an involuntary manner by use of intimidation or threats or some other form of pressure or force. It involves a set of various types of forceful actions that violate the free will of an individual to induce a desired response, usually having a strict choice or option against a person in such a way a victim cannot escape. John and Carl Whaley tried to get me to sign an unfair buyout agreement and they refused to let me into the business bank account unless I signed this unfair buyout agreement. Alliance Bank & Trust would not let me back into the Alliance Bank & Trust Fisher Rx Direct business bank account unless I signed this unfair buyout agreement also, so they were guilty of coercion. I did not sign it but they tried to use intimidation to get me to sign it. Alliance Bank & Trust backed John and Carl Whaley because John Whaley was on the Board of Directors of Alliance Bank & Trust.

III. Community Pharmacy

A. Conversion

The tort of conversion occurs when the defendant so substantially interferes with the plaintiff's possession or ownership of property that it is fair to require the defendant to pay the property's full value. See Rest. 2d §222A. It is irrelevant that the defendant did not know that the action would constitute a tort or a crime. Thus in the law of intentional torts, "ignorance of the law is no excuse." Community Pharmacy committed conversion when it purchased stolen property from John and Carl Whaley. John and Carl Whaley did not have the legal authority to sell my fifty percent ownership of Fisher Rx Direct. Community Pharmacy did not ask for my agreement to purchase my fifty percent ownership in Fisher Rx Direct. I would have agreed but Community Pharmacy would have written 2 different checks for the purchase of patient files and other assets of Fisher Rx Direct. Community Pharmacy should have written a check to me and to John and Carl Whaley. As far as I am concerned Community Pharmacy owes me for my fifty percent ownership of Fisher Rx Direct patient files and other assets. Receipt of stolen property is punished as larceny in North Carolina.

B. Interference with Existing Contracts

Community Pharmacy interfered with existing contracts of Fisher Rx Direct when Community Pharmacy bought the patient files and other assets of Fisher Rx Direct. My fifty percent of the patient files and other assets of Fisher Rx Direct was sold to Community Pharmacy without my authorization. Community Pharmacy should have checked with me before buying anything from Fisher Rx Direct. This occurs when defendant induces another to breach a contract with the plaintiff. I believe agreeing to purchase my fifty percent of patient files and other assets of Fisher Rx Direct helped the Whaleys to breach their contract with me.

C. Interference with Prospective Advantage

This tort occurs when interference with future contracts is interfered with by the defendant. This occurred when Community Pharmacy purchased my fifty percent of patient files and other assets of Fisher Rx Direct without my permission. John and Carl Whaley stole my fifty percent of patient files and other assets of Fisher Rx Direct and sold them to Community Pharmacy, which means that Community Pharmacy bought stolen property. In North Carolina, constructive possession is sufficient for larceny.

D. Negligent Infliction of Emotional Distress
Under the tort of negligence the defendant has imposed an unreasonable risk of harm on the plaintiff and the plaintiff is injured as a result. As a business, Community Pharmacy should have known they had to verify everything with me because I owned fifty percent of Fisher Rx Direct. In my opinion, this was carelessness on the part of Community Pharmacy. The harm that resulted in the

negligence of Community Pharmacy, was that I was never reimbursed for my fifty percent ownership of the patient files and other assets of Community Pharmacy. The courts use a balancing test, if the harm to another from defendant's conduct is greater than the utility of that conduct, the risk is deemed unreasonable. All Community Pharmacy had to do was contact me. I would have consented to sell but required them to write me a check for my half of the Fisher Rx Direct patient files and other assets.

IV. Thomas Norkus

A. Fraud and/or larceny by trick

Thomas Norkus committed fraud against Mutual Drug of NC and against me. In September of 2011 he tried to open his own pharmacy but his financing fell thru. He was able to get a permit and did find a place to rent. He did all this before finding out that his financing fell through. He should have secured the financing, then obtained the permit. Remember, that I did open my own pharmacy successfully, but I chose the wrong partners. In November 2011, he applied to open an account with NC Mutual Drug. In December 2011, he received his account number from NC Mutual Drug. The name of his company was Josepharm. Shortly after he received his NC Mutual Drug account number, he began returning outdated drugs to NC Mutual Drug. He never purchased the drugs from NC Mutual Drug and requested the credit be applied to his account at Mutual Drug. He tried to obtain money from Drugs he did not purchase from NC Mutual Drug, and that is fraud. He tried to receive money or credit from NC Mutual Drug for drugs he supposedly received thru bartering with pharmacies he had worked at in the past. It was over $2000 worth of drugs he sent to NC Mutual Drug and that is considered a felony because it involved over $1000 worth of merchandise. He almost lost his pharmacy license because of this activity. I did help him find an attorney to take the case. My attorney I used for the Board concerning my business refused to take his case, and said he needed to hire a criminal attorney. Let me just say I have a soft heart and I was thinking he just did something stupid and because he got caught he would never do it again. Obviously I was wrong because he committed fraud against me as described below. I always like to give everyone the benefit of the doubt and make my own decision. When he finally told me about his trouble with the board he started crying and this caused me to really feel compassion for him.

The name of the woman Tom committed adultery with is Emily Williams. She is the wife of David Williams. Currently Mrs. Williams is an online copywriter for Lowe's Companies in Charlotte, Contributing Writer for Epicurean Charlotte, works for the Catholic News and Herald as a correspondent and an editor for Crossroads Magazine at Belmont Abbey College. She was formerly an English Lecturer at Belmont Abbey College. David Williams is the Vice President of Academic Affairs and Dean of the faculty at Belmont Abbey College. Mrs. Williams is almost 30 years younger than Tom. I am almost ten years younger than Tom.

I had let it be known to Tom if he wanted to start seeing other people that I would move out. He chose to keep the adulterous affair with Emily Williams a secret, so I would not leave him, and I would continue to spend money on him and his house. I had also placed Tom on my bank account before I found out that he was cheating on me. However, I took Tom off my bank account and no longer allowed him to use my car when I found out he was cheating on me. I would have moved out the night I discovered he was cheating on me if he had not indicated to me that he would move out. Actually, he indicated to me that he would move to Cary, NC because that is where he is working now. He did not move out, so I did.

Tom committed fraud (tort of common law deceit) when he allowed me to believe he was being faithful to me and let me continue to spend money on him and his house. Under criminal law, that is larceny by trick. He has reimbursed me for close to

$4500 of the money I spent on him and his house last year. He still owes me in excess of $10,000. Mrs. Emily Williams and William Joe Goodman conspired with Tom to cover up the crime of adultery between Mrs. Williams and Tom. This cover-up led to me being a victim of fraud and/or larceny by trick.

B. Intentional Infliction of Emotional Distress

In my opinion, the actions of Tom came about because I refused to share his bed unless I married him. I made sure he was aware of this before we started dating. He agreed to this or we would not have started dating each other. This tort is usually defined as the intentional or reckless infliction, by extreme or outrageous conduct, of severe or mental distress even in the absence of physical harm. According to the second restatement, there are 3 possible mental states on defendant's part, any of these will qualify: Defendant desires to cause the plaintiff emotional distress; knows with substantial certainty that the plaintiff will suffer emotional distress; and recklessly disregards that emotional distress will occur. The third restatement's definition says that a person recklessly causes harm if: the person knows of the risk of harm created by his conduct, or knows facts that make that risk obvious to anyone in the actor's situation; and the precaution that would eliminate or reduce that risk involves burdens that are so slight relative to the magnitude of the risk as to render highly blameworthy the actor's failure to adopt the precaution. Tom knew that I would consider his conduct extreme and outrageous because we were dating and sharing a house. He had the adulterous affair in the house I was sharing with him. Tom also knew how I felt about adultery and everything that had happened to me in my recent past and he committed the actions against me anyway. He did not want me to find out about his cheating because he told me after I caught him, that I would not have known anything if I had not had the security cameras installed.   He should not have been cheating on me and I would not have anything to catch him doing. I was the one doing his laundry, having his house cleaned, and cooking for him.   I was also spending quite a bit of money on his house, because I considered it our home. I considered the money I spent as an investment in our relationship. I was also the one that paid for all of our dates unless it was my birthday. I was able to get some of the money back I spent on Tom and his house last year. I found out that he took Mrs. Williams to his parent's 60th wedding anniversary. That was disrespectful to me and to his parents. His parents are strong Catholics and would not understand one of their son's having an adulterous affair because he was raised as a Catholic. I converted to Catholicism in April 2012. Marriage is a major sacrament in the Catholic religion. Of course, it is important in all religions. Tom and I were not married, but I would have been willing to marry him if he had not cheated on me. The cheating itself was bad enough but the fact that he cheated with a married woman was even worse because he proved to me that he does not respect the sacrament of marriage like I do. He also proved to me that he lies to his family as well as everyone else. When Tom committed his actions, he knew how it would affect me and he did not care. His actions not only hurt me but David Williams, her husband as well.

I was physically hurt as well because now I am on 2 blood pressure medicines and a drug that helps patients deal with posttraumatic stress. I am doing better because of the Lord. He is helping me deal with everything thru my writing. In my opinion, the adulterous conduct of Tom and Mrs. Williams was both a public and private nuisance. Their actions were a private nuisance because my own home was used for the adulterous relationship between my boyfriend and Mrs. Williams. He is my ex-boyfriend now, of course. Their actions were a public nuisance because adultery hurts the public, especially the families. Each and every person that commits adultery hurts the public.

C. Extortion/Blackmail

Tom conspired with William Joe Goodman to trick me into paying the extortion money that Joe was extorting from Tom and me in order to get Joe to move out of our house. Well it was actually Tom's house but we were dating and I did consider it our house. Joe would not leave peacefully unless Tom and I paid him $750 to leave. I paid it and I had no clue that Tom was cheating on me with Mrs. Williams at that time or that Joe knew and never told me. He actually did tell me when he made it out of jail but I did not believe him because I knew he was being vindictive because neither Tom nor I bailed him out of jail. He owed both Tom and myself money. He was actually getting free rent from Tom in order to help Tom cover up his cheating on me with Mrs. Williams. Tom was guilty of conspiring with Joe to extort money from me to get Joe out the house. I found out that Tom was cheating on me at the end of September.

V.   David and Emily Williams

A. Adultery

Emily Williams committed adultery with my boyfriend. Tom and I were not married but we talked about marriage before we started dating. I would have been willing to marry him eventually if he had not cheated on me. Emily Williams is married to David Williams, and she cheated on her husband with my boyfriend at our house. The dysfunctional relationship between David Williams and his wife Mrs. Williams affected my life and it should not have. Tom should not have cheated on me and Mrs. Williams should have honored her marriage vows.

As far as I know, David Williams has always been faithful to his wife. The reason I included him in the complaint was because Tom told me that he knew. I do not think he knew and that Tom was lying to me. In my opinion, Tom is a pathological liar and can't be trusted. Of course, finding out that, David Williams is the Vice President of Academic Affairs and the Dean of the Faculty at Belmont Abbey

College helped me realize that Tom lied to me about that, but I was making sure all my bases were covered. Mr. Williams now knows about the adulterous relationship that his wife was having with my boyfriend because I told him. His response to me was to never contact him again or it would be harassment. I do not think he believed me at first but he does now. David Williams could not control the behavior of his wife Emily Williams. A legal competent adult cannot be responsible for the actions of another legal competent adult unless coercion is used.

B. Fraud

Emily Williams was guilty of fraud because she conspired with Tom to keep her adulterous relationship a secret from me. Under tort law, it does not matter how unlikely the consequence of his or her action is, the defendant is still liable. Mrs. Williams chose to have an adulterous relationship with my boyfriend Tom. When she chose to cheat on her husband, she should have realized that Tom was not a trustworthy person because he was cheating on me, with her. As I stated earlier, he is my ex-boyfriend now. Remember, she technically committed fraud against her husband when she had an adulterous relationship with my then boyfriend Tom.

C. Negligent Infliction of Emotional Distress

The tort of negligence occurs when the conduct of the defendant imposes an unreasonable risk upon the plaintiff, resulting in an injury to the plaintiff. The defendant's mental state is irrelevant. Adultery is a public and private nuisance. Adultery hurts the public because of immoral behavior and the private individual because of the same reason. Any person who commits adultery is very selfish because the person does not care how her or his action affects the life of another person. Emily Williams' adulterous relationship with my boyfriend Thomas Norkus affected my life and she did not care how it affected my life. Thomas Norkus was just as guilty as Emily

Williams because of his behavior and he was one of the plaintiff's in the lawsuit. Thomas Norkus did not care how his selfish behavior affected me or David Williams. Both Thomas Norkus and Emily Williams put their own desires before the Lord, which means they listened to the deceptions of Satan.

There are five parts for a prime facie case for negligence and they are: duty, failure to conform to duty, causation in fact, proximate cause, and actual damage. As a married woman Emily Williams owed a legal duty to the public and especially her husband, to conduct herself in a moral way, so as not to break the adultery law in NC. And of course to commit the mortal sin of adultery. Adultery encompasses the cardinal sins of lust, gluttony, greed, sloth, envy, and pride. Sloth can mean spiritual laziness as well as physical laziness. Pride is included because you are not honoring the Lord. The sins of lust, gluttony, greed, and envy include putting the desires of oneself above others including the Lord. The actions of Mrs. Williams have proven that she is guilty of the mortal sin and cardinal sins previously mentioned. Mrs. Williams has a lot to make up for if she can swallow her pride. She did not want to apologize to me as part of the settlement I asked for, so I am sure Mrs. Williams has too much pride. Mrs. Williams needs to humble herself before God and I do not know if she can. Several people think that being humble means being weak. That is not the case, if you can humble yourself before God, that means being strong. Mrs. Williams failed to conform her conduct to the standard set by the adultery law in North Carolina and the Bible. Mrs. Williams adulterous relationship with Thomas Norkus was the cause in fact of the financial and physical harm caused to me. Mrs. Williams failed to act with reasonable care and her actions caused harm to a child of God. There is a sufficiently close connection or causal link between Mrs. Williams act of negligence and the harm that I suffered. I suffered actual physical and financial harm because of Mrs. Williams' adulterous relationship with my boyfriend Thomas Norkus. Remember, Tom is my ex-boyfriend now.

VI.   William Joe Goodman

A. Battery

Battery is the intentional infliction of a harmful or offensive bodily contact. No intent to harm is necessary. Joe did intent to harm me last year; Joe pinched me really hard by twisting a small piece of my skin while pinching me. I am comparing it to a torture technique. He hurt me very much when he did this and he did it deliberately. I did tell Tom about this but that is all. I almost went to the police about what he had done and I wish now I had. Also, remember that ignorance of the law is no excuse, in the law of intentional torts.

B. Fraud

William Joe Goodman always went by Joe as far as I know. Tom allowed Joe to move in January 2014. I had no clue about this until I had already moved in. Joe was always late on his rent. He was actually late on his rent as soon as he moved in. According to Tom, he let Joe move in because he was scared and could not find a regular job. I kept on telling him over and over to trust the Lord and he did not. Joe cost Tom a lot of money when we finally were able to kick him out. Joe helped Tom keep his adulterous relationship with Emily Williams hidden from me, because Joe knew keeping Tom's cheating a secret from me would allow him a free place to live. And it did for a few months, until Joe wound up in jail. Joe was just as guilty of fraud as Tom because Joe was an accomplice of Tom's.

In my opinion, Joe was always out for himself only. He is an extremely selfish and vindictive person, who does not care about anyone but himself. I met Joe before he moved in and he tried to get Tom and I to let him move in then. We both tried to blow him off and it did not work. Tom and I were trying to be polite without being rude, but neither of us wanted Joe there. Tom realized his mistake as soon as Joe moved in. I never trusted Joe because he knew that neither Tom nor I wanted him to move in, but he was able to get to Tom when I was not around. Joe knew that we were trying to blow him off without being rude, but he did not care. And of course, Tom did not let me know about Joe, until after I had already moved in. That was not good either and did throw up a red flag. However, I did decide to give Tom the benefit of the doubt because I knew he was scared financially. However, I was still angry at him for his actions in this instance. Another reason, I did not leave when I found out about Joe, is that I did not trust Joe, I never trusted Joe and if there was a way I could help Tom get rid of Joe, I wanted to.

C. Intentional Infliction of Emotional Distress

William Joe Goodman intentionally wanted to hurt me and was extremely spiteful about it. Tom finally kicked Joe out of our house when Joe was arrested by the Charlotte police. He was facing charges of failure to appear, failure to pay a fare on the light rail, and public drunkenness. Neither Tom nor I were willing to help Joe because he owed us both money. I did not like Joe and did not trust Joe and I think Tom finally felt the same way.

Joe's conduct against me was extreme and outrageous because Tom was kicking him out and letting me stay. Also, we did not help Joe out of jail. Joe told me after he was able to get out of jail that Tom had been cheating on me for months. He said he had an epiphany while in jail and the Lord told him to tell me this. I did not believe him because of the way he went about it. I did find out that Tom had been cheating on me with a married woman after I caught him with her on our security cameras. I figured that Joe was partially lying and partially telling the truth, after I found that Tom was cheating on me. I also figured out that Joe had been blackmailing Tom for free rent in order to keep the adulterous relationship he was having with Mrs. Emily Williams hidden from me. Joe wanted to make sure he hurt me anyway possible and he did say several awful things to me. Then he tried to get me to be his roommate, I do not think so. I might be naïve but I am not stupid. I would have believed him but he kept on embellishing his story and tried to get me to let him move in with me when I left Tom. As far as I was concerned he was trying to help himself again by breaking up me and Tom. Tom's actions broke us up, not what Joe told me. I will be honest, I became suspicious of Tom after Joe told me he was cheating on me, but I had to let the Lord prove it to me and I knew he would not use Joe but would let me know in a better way.

D. Extortion/Blackmail

Joe blackmailed Tom for free rent to keep the adulterous affair between Tom and Mrs. Emily Williams hidden from me. Joe also extorted $750 from me and Tom to move out quickly. Tom let me pay for it and he was cheating on me then. That was larceny by trick (fraud) then by Joe and Tom. Tom did pay me back the $750 that Joe extorted from us. As well as some of the money I spent on him and his house. Joe extorted free rent from Tom and as well as the money he extorted from me and Tom to get him to move out quickly. The extortion/blackmail schemes of Joe against Tom and I are felonies in NC because of the amount of money involved. Joe owed Tom over $2000 in rent when he moved out plus the $750 he extorted from us to move.

VII. Criminal Issues

Felonies in NC are crimes punished by death or imprisoned for greater than a year. The crimes committed against me include solicitation, attempt, conspiracy, larceny, false pretenses, and embezzlement. Also, the crimes committed against me include both misdemeanors and felonies. Remember until convicted in a court of law crimes are considered alleged. However, I am providing proof of all crimes as much as possible and I have contacted the appropriate authorities to have everyone investigated that is allegedly involved in the crimes. I pray that each person that I am alleging that is guilty of the specific crimes mentioned receive fines, community service, imprisonment, and/or restitution. We will see what happens and I will update all of my nonfiction books that are dealing with the crimes when available. Of course, the updates will be free.

Embezzlement is the fraudulent conversion of the personal property of another by a person in lawful possession of that property. Solicitation is inciting, counseling, advising, urging, or commanding another to commit the crime. It is not necessary that the person solicited actually respond affirmatively. Conspiracy is an agreement between two or more persons with an intent to enter into an agreement to achieve the objective of the agreement. No overt act required in furtherance require under NC common law. Conspirators are liable for foreseeable crimes committed by other conspirators in furtherance of the conspiracy. In NC, attempt is an act done with the intent to commit a crime that falls short of committing the crime. An overt act beyond mere preparation required. NC uses the proximity test for attempt. Please remember, a person cannot attempt a criminally negligent act.

A. John and Carl Whaley

Embezzlement in NC concerning a business in NC is defined as the following:

1. § 14-97. Appropriation of partnership funds by partner to personal use.

   Any person engaged in a partnership business in the State of North Carolina who shall, without the knowledge and consent of his copartner or copartners, take funds belonging to the partnership business and appropriate the same to his own personal use with the fraudulent intent of depriving his copartners of the use thereof, shall be guilty of a felony. Appropriation of partnership funds with a value of one hundred thousand dollars ($100,000) or more by a partner is a Class C felony. Appropriation of partnership funds with the value of less than one hundred thousand dollars ($100,000) by a partner is a Class H felony. (1921, c. 127; C.S., s. 4274(a); 1993, c. 539, s. 1179; 1994, Ex. Sess., c. 24, s. 14(c); 1997-443, s. 19.25(i).)

John and Carl Whaley sold patient files and other assets of Fisher Rx Direct. Carl and John Whaley them pocketed the money. I believe that the patient files and other assets of Fisher Rx Direct was sold for $300,000 or more and I was supposed to get half of that. I am not even sure exactly how much the patient files and other assets were sold for because I was never told. I am also wondering how they were able to sell anything without my signature. I never signed anything which allowed them to sell my fifty percent ownership of the patient files and other assets of Fisher Rx Direct. The District Attorney can subpoena this information from John and Carl Whaley, Community Pharmacy, and/or Alliance Bank & Trust for the bank records. Because of the issues involved the District Attorney should be able to subpoena all bank records held by John, Carl, and Harriet Whaley. The bank records of Shelia Cooper should also be subpoenaed because she is a conspirator in the crimes of the Whaley's against me. Any potential bank account that the Whaley's could hide stolen funds can be subpoenaed I think. Even if the stolen funds are hidden overseas, the Whaleys have enough assets in the United States which can be seized to cover fines and restitution. Other crimes committed by the Whaleys include solicitation, attempt, conspiracy, and false pretenses. If my signature was on paperwork for the selling of the Fisher Rx Direct patient files and other assets, then my signature was a forgery.

Which means the Whaleys are also guilty of forgery. Shelia Cooper and Harriet Whaley were solicited and became guilty of attempt and conspiracy also. John and Carl Whaley solicited Shelia Cooper and Harriet Whaley. Harriet Whaley is the wife of John Whaley and mother of Carl Whaley. Shelia Cooper worked for John and Carl Whaley. She also worked for Fisher Rx Direct but disobeyed a direct order from me and I fired her. John and Carl Whaley let her continue to work for them at Fisher Rx Direct after I fired her. John and Carl Whaley kept me out of Fisher Rx Direct illegally. I tried to legally get Fisher Rx Direct back under my control and that is when they sold the patients and other assets and pocketed the money. John and Carl Whaley also refused to return my personal stuff that I had left at Fisher Rx Direct. The District Attorney is currently investigating the actions of Carl and John Whaley in this situation. Remember, there are no statute of limitations for felonies in NC. I exhausted my civil remedies before I filed criminal complaints against the people that wronged me civilly and criminally. The Whaley's attempted coercion against me, when they tried to make me sign an illegal contract. I was forced into Bankruptcy because of the actions of John and Carl Whaley. Carl and John Whaley settled with my bankruptcy trustee. My bankruptcy trustee settled civilly with Carl and John Whaley, the civil settlement did not include a settlement of any of the criminal actions of John and Carl Whaley. If I was given my half of the sell concerning the patient files and other assets of Fisher Rx Direct, I would not have had to declare bankruptcy and I would not have lost my house. John and Carl Whaley are guilty of embezzlement, fraud, bribery, extortion, and obstruction of justice and they have committed at least two acts and they conspired with each other and others. I have turned everything over to the Shelby Police Department and the Shelby Police Department has turned everything over to the Cleveland County District Attorney.

B. Alliance Bank and Trust

Alliance Bank & Trust conspired with Carl and John Whaley to deprive me of my fifty percent ownership of Fisher Rx Direct because John Whaley is on the Board of Directors of Alliance Bank & Trust. I have exhausted all civil legal remedies that I am aware of against Alliance Bank & Trust. I did that before I filed a criminal complaint against everyone involved in my civil lawsuit. A company can be charged with a crime because the acts of employees and the acts of members of the company's Board of Directors. Companies can be criminally fined and put on probation. No company wants a judge as an overseer. In my opinion, Alliance Bank & Trust is guilty of embezzlement, conspiracy, and attempt because Alliance Bank & Trust did what John Whaley solicited them to do. The District Attorney can impose fines and probation on Alliance Bank & Trust because of their actions against me. Alliance Bank & Trust is guilty of attempted coercion when they would not allow be back into the Fisher Rx Bank business bank account because I would not sign an unfair and illegal contract.

A contract is illegal if it involves doing something that is a criminal act, a civil wrong, or against the public good. A contract whose purpose is to get the party to it to break another legally binding contract that the party has made already is also illegal. The Courts will not enforce an illegal contract. The illegal contract that he the Whaleys and Alliance Bank & Trust tried to coerce me into signing was illegal because it would tried to rewrite the original buy and sell agreement between me and Whaley Communications (John and Carl Whaley).

By attributing the acts and intentions of the company's employees to the company itself, an approach the Supreme Court first endorsed in the 1909 case of **_New York Central and Hudson River Railroad Co. v. United States_**. That case held that since corporations were already liable in *civil* cases for their board of directors or employees' bad conduct (within the scope of their job), it was perfectly appropriate to extend that rule to the criminal law. But why seek criminal sanctions against a company rather than civil ones? One reason is the power of a grand jury. In a civil proceeding, a person can bring its attorneys to any employee deposition, and the proceeding's scope is limited to the misdeeds alleged in the complaint. But in a criminal grand jury investigation, prosecutors can use subpoenas to force employees to testify—with no company lawyer at their side. Remember, John Whaley used his position on the Board of Directors of Alliance Bank & Trust to get an employee to do his dirty work for him. The name of the person I know of off the top of my head is Kelly Young. She was the branch manager of the Alliance Bank & Trust located in Shelby, NC. I think the actions of Alliance Bank & Trust against me can come under RICO violations because John Whaley is on the Board of Directors of Alliance Bank & Trust and used the bank for his own criminal activity.

C. Community Pharmacy

Under NC law, receipt of stolen property can be punished as larceny. Receiving possession and control of stolen property know to have been obtained in a manner constituting a criminal offense by another person with the intent to permanently deprive the owner of her interest in it. Constructive possession is sufficient. Community Pharmacy should have known that my signature was needed to buy my fifty percent ownership of Fisher Rx Direct patient files and other assets. I had no clue when the patient files and other assets of Fisher Rx Direct was sold to Community Pharmacy because I was not told anything. I also was not told the amount that the patient files or other assets were sold for. I had asked for a copy of the check written by Community Pharmacy to John and Carl Whaley and I have never received a copy of the check or contract under which the patient files or other assets were sold to Community Pharmacy. I did file a civil complaint against Community Pharmacy to get the information I wanted and they refused to give it to me also. However, the Bankruptcy Court is now handling my lawsuit against Community Pharmacy because it is considered an asset of my bankrupt estate. I do have a bankruptcy attorney handling this. This was handled in part Pro Se and in part by my bankruptcy attorney. I do not know if the actions of Community Pharmacy can be prosecuted under RICO. However, I know that they bought stolen property and they are guilty of obstruction of justice because of the refusal to give me a copy of the check written for Fisher Rx Direct patient files and other assets and refused to give a copy of the contract that they bought the patient files and other assets of Fisher Rx Direct. I do know that if the District Attorney can make a case of at 2 acts of racketeering activity he can make a case. I think the conspiracy between Community Pharmacy and the Whaleys can make that case.

D. Thomas Norkus

The criminal issues of Thomas Norkus are adultery, and fraud (larceny by trick). Tom committed fraud against NC Mutual Drug and me. The adultery he committed against David Williams and he committed the adultery with Emily Williams. Adultery is a class 2 misdemeanor in North Carolina. The fraud against NC Mutual Drug and myself are felonies because both involve money and/or merchandise obtained by fraudulent means of over a $1000. The adultery he committed with Emily Williams led to fraud being committed against me. Emily Williams is a married woman and she is married to David Williams. Under NC law, both parties are equally guilty, whether or not you are the married party. Joe blackmailed Tom to receive free rent. I had no clue that Tom was cheating on me because I was out of town a lot working for us. Tom knew I was working for us and he let me continue to pay for our dates and groceries. He also let me pay for work on the house and to have the house cleaned while he was cheating on me. Furthermore, he let me do his laundry or have it done and cook for him while he was cheating on me. I should have charged him my hourly rate as a pharmacist for cooking and doing his laundry for him. Actually, I had the house cleaned for him, I did not do that myself. However, I did do his laundry for him. The offering or taking a bribe in NC may constitute a crime and considered a felony. I think in this instant it is a felony because he was bribing Joe to cover up his adulterous relationship with Emily Williams. The adultery is a crime in NC. The cover up resulted in a felony being committed against me. The felony is considered false pretenses and/or larceny by trick. He allowed me to put him on my bank account while he was cheating on me as well as spending money on him and his house. I was able to get back thru the civil court system some of the money I spent on him and his house last year but not all of it. I have turned everything over to the financial crimes unit of the Charlotte Mecklenburg Police Department. The actions of Thomas Norkus against me and others prove that he is an extremely selfish person and does not care about anyone but himself.

Tom did try to start his own pharmacy with funds he tried to obtain fraudulently from NC Mutual Drug. He obtained drugs illegally and tried to return them to NC Mutual Drug to try and obtain financial credit from NC Mutual Drug. He did not obtain the drugs he sent back to NC Mutual Drug legally from Mutual Drug. He also did not have the proper paperwork. Because Tom did not have the proper paperwork, it meant he obtained the drugs in an illegal manner and that resulted in fraud against NC Mutual Drug. Tom almost lost his pharmacy license because of this illegal activity. Tom was disciplined by the NC and SC Pharmacy boards because of his fraud against NC Mutual Drug. I do think the District Attorney can discover evidence of crimes that are at least 2 in the last ten years concerning the actions of Thomas Norkus. I have actually stated the proof in the book and I do have the evidence. The evidence against Tom involves copies of checks and my bank account and I will not put that in this book.

E. Emily and David Williams

David Williams is the husband of Emily Williams. I do not think he is guilty of any crime unless he really did know about the adulterous relationship with my boyfriend Thomas Norkus. As I have stated before he is my ex-boyfriend now. I do not know why Tom told me that her husband knew. I guess maybe to try and get me from telling him. It did not work, instead I made David Williams part of my lawsuit. If David Williams knew he is as guilty as Tom of fraud and/or larceny by trick committed against me. I do not think Mr. Williams knew and I am not sure he believed me when I told him that his wife Emily Williams was involved in an adulterous relationship with my boyfriend Tom Norkus. Of course I am sure he believes me now.

Emily Williams was committing adultery with my boyfriend Tom Norkus in our house. Her actions have proven that she is an extremely selfish person and does not care about anyone but herself. She did not think how her actions affected anyone else and she did not know that her actions is considered a crime in NC. The cover up of the adultery by Emily Williams resulted in the crime of fraud and/or larceny by trick being committed against me. Under tort law, ignorance of the law is no excuse and a conspirator is responsible for any foreseeable crimes committed by other conspirators in furtherance of the conspiracy. I think the District Attorney can make a case for RICO violations because of her conspiring with Tom to cover-up her adulterous relationship with Tom. She also conspired with Tom to keep the adulterous relationship secret from her husband. Emily Williams is guilty of 2 or more acts of racketeering activity in a 10 year period.

F. William Joe Goodman

William Joe Goodman committed battery and extortion against me. Joe committed extortion and/or blackmail against Tom. Joe blackmailed Tom for free rent in order to hide the adulterous affair that Tom Norkus was having with Mrs. Williams. Joe thought he had it made until he was arrested and went to jail because of trespass, failure to appear, and public drunkenness. Tom did evict him when he found out Joe was in jail. I wanted Joe evicted because I did not trust him and with good reason. The fact that Joe helped Tom hide the adulterous relationship he was having with Emily Williams, made him an accomplice in all the actions civil and criminal against me. He did extort $750 from me and Tom to move out quicker. We could have still evicted him but it would have taken a lot longer. Actually, it was originally going to be less than $750, but Joe kept increasing the amount he wanted. Honestly, I had to go to a motel to stay away from Joe, because I was afraid of him since I knew he was desperate. I am the one that paid Joe the extortion money to Joe to get him to move out. Tom did pay me back the extortion money and about $3500 of the money I spent on him and his house in 2014. Joe is guilty of 2 or more acts of racketeering activity in a 10 year period.

VIII. Conclusion

The writing of this book has helped tremendously. I pray that it helps others, especially in their spiritual journey. John and Carl Whaley broke the original purchase/sell agreement when they illegally kept me out of Fisher Rx Direct. Then Carl and John Whaley tried to coerce me into signing an illegal contract, in which they actually did a complete rewrite of the original purchase/sell agreement. The Whaleys own lawyer drew up the original purchase/sell agreement in which they bought fifty percent of Fisher Rx Direct. Before I signed the contract, I did read it. I knew that if the contract protected them that it protected me because it was a fifty/fifty contract. John and Carl Whaley never owned a hundred percent of Fisher Rx Direct. Of course, the purchase/sell contract between us, did not stop John and Carl Whaley from doing their illegal acts. From what I understand, John Whaley controlled his family. Unfortunately, under the law each person is responsible for his or her own acts unless coercion can be proven. I do not know if John Whaley used coercion to get Harriet Whaley or Carl Whaley to commit illegal acts. The District Attorney can find that out. The actions of Shelia Cooper are being investigated also. I do not know if she was coerced or acted of her own free will.

Tom Norkus used me, lied to me, cheated on me, and essentially stole from me. I do not know what will happen to him. Tom Norkus and Emily Williams should both be charged with adultery.

At the least, the District Attorney can make each of them pay a $1000 fine to the state. I do continue to pray for his salvation each and every day. I do still love him and always will, but he has proven to me he is not an honest person. He only cares about himself. And always puts himself above others, including the Lord. I do think he can redeem himself thru the Lord, if he wants to. However, he committed crimes against NC Mutual Drug and against me and I think the District Attorney of Mecklenburg County should step up in this situation. In my opinion, the District Attorney could assess fines against Tom and make Tom do Community Service. I think restitution to me might be in order also. Tom owes me about $11,000. I spent in excess of $15000 dollars on Tom and his house in 2014. I was living with Tom in 2014 but was not sharing his bed because we were not married. Tom knew about my religious views before we started dating. If he had let me know that he did respect marriage before we started dating, I would not have started dating him. I love Tom and I always will. I have told Tom this and I have let him know each and every mistake he make with me. I did sue him and won, by getting some of the money back I spent on him and his house in 2014. I would have been willing to marry Tom until he decided to cheat on me. The issues I have with Tom is more than a boyfriend cheating on a girlfriend it involved crimes and criminal conspiracy.

I believe the District Attorney of Mecklenburg County can bring charges under the US and NC RICO statutes because of the relationship Tom, Joe, and Mrs. Williams had with each other. I was the victim of all the criminal activity. The prize for Tom was my continued financial support as long as I did not find out he was cheating on me. He had Joe and Mrs. Williams, helping him cover up his actions. Each person is guilty of 2 more acts of racketeering activity in a 10 year period.

I think the District Attorneys of Cleveland County NC and Mecklenburg County might be able to use the United States and North Carolina RICO states under all crimes committed against me discussed in this book. The **Racketeer Influenced and Corrupt Organizations Act**, commonly referred to as the **RICO Act** or simply **RICO**, is a **United States federal law** that provides for extended criminal penalties and a civil **cause of action** for acts performed as part of an ongoing **criminal organization**,. The RICO Act focuses specifically on **racketeering**, and it allows the *leaders* of a syndicate to be tried for the crimes which they *ordered* others to do **or assisted them in doing**, closing a perceived loophole that allowed a person who instructed someone else to, for example, murder, to be exempt from the trial because he did not actually commit the crime personally. Under RICO, a person who has committed "at least two acts of racketeering activity" drawn from a list of 35 crimes—27 **federal crimes** and 8 **state crimes**—within a 10-year period can be charged with **racketeering** if such acts are related in one of four specified ways to an "enterprise". Those found guilty of racketeering can be fined up to $25,000 and sentenced to 20 years in prison per racketeering count. In addition, the racketeer must forfeit all ill-gotten gains and interest in any business gained through a pattern of "racketeering activity." RICO also permits a private individual "damaged in his business or property" by a "racketeer" to file a civil suit. The plaintiff must prove the existence of an "enterprise". The defendant(s) are not the enterprise; in other words, the defendant(s) and the enterprise are not one and the same.[3] There must be one of four specified relationships between the defendant(s) and the enterprise: either the defendant(s) invested the proceeds of the pattern of racketeering activity into the enterprise (18 U.S.C. § 1962(a)); or the defendant(s) acquired or maintained an interest in, or control of, the enterprise through the pattern of racketeering activity (subsection (b)); or the defendant(s) conducted or participated in the affairs of the enterprise "through" the pattern of racketeering activity (subsection (c)); or the defendant(s) conspired to do one of the above (subsection (d)).[4] In essence, the enterprise is either the 'prize,' 'instrument,' 'victim,' or 'perpetrator' of the racketeers. A civil RICO action can be filed in state or federal court.

Both the criminal and civil components allow the recovery of triple damage (damages in triple the amount of actual/compensatory damages).

Before each civil or criminal action I commenced I prayed to the Lord. Make sure the Lord is guiding you in every endeavor.

References

1. *Emanuel, Steven L. (2011-04-05). Emanuel Law Outlines: Torts Keyed to Prosser Wade Schwartz Kelly & Partlett 12th Edition (Kindle Locations 4928-4930). Aspen Publishers (Wolters Kluwer Legal). Kindle Edition.*

2. *Emanuel, Steven L. (2011-04-05). Emanuel Law Outlines: Torts Keyed to Prosser Wade Schwartz Kelly & Partlett 12th Edition (Kindle Locations 17533-17534). Aspen Publishers (Wolters Kluwer Legal). Kindle Edition.*

3. *Emanuel, Steven L. (2011-04-05). Emanuel Law Outlines: Torts Keyed to Prosser Wade Schwartz Kelly & Partlett 12th Edition*

(Kindle Locations 16378-16385). Aspen Publishers (Wolters Kluwer Legal). Kindle Edition. Emanuel, Steven L. (2011-04-05). Emanuel Law Outlines: Torts Keyed to Prosser Wade Schwartz Kelly & Partlett 12th Edition (Kindle Locations 16167-16170). Aspen Publishers (Wolters Kluwer Legal). Kindle Edition. Emanuel, Steven L. (2011-04-05). Emanuel Law Outlines: Torts Keyed to Prosser Wade Schwartz Kelly & Partlett 12th Edition (Kindle Locations 16163-16164). Aspen Publishers (Wolters Kluwer Legal). Kindle Edition.

4. *Emanuel, Steven L. (2011-04-05). Emanuel Law Outlines: Torts Keyed to Prosser Wade Schwartz Kelly & Partlett 12th Edition (Kindle Locations 17295-17298). Aspen Publishers (Wolters Kluwer Legal). Kindle Edition.*

5. *Emanuel, Steven L. (2011-04-05). Emanuel Law Outlines: Torts Keyed to Prosser Wade Schwartz Kelly & Partlett 12th Edition (Kindle Locations 17275-17279). Aspen Publishers (Wolters Kluwer Legal). Kindle Edition.*

6. Emanuel, Steven L. (2011-04-05). *Emanuel Law Outlines: Torts Keyed to Prosser Wade Schwartz Kelly & Partlett 12th Edition* (Kindle Locations 17271-17275). Aspen Publishers (Wolters Kluwer Legal). Kindle Edition

7. Emanuel, Steven L. (2011-04-05). *Emanuel Law Outlines: Torts Keyed to Prosser Wade Schwartz Kelly & Partlett 12th Edition* (Kindle Locations 17361-17363). Aspen Publishers (Wolters Kluwer Legal). Kindle Edition.

8. Emanuel, Steven L. (2011-04-05). *Emanuel Law Outlines: Torts Keyed to Prosser Wade Schwartz Kelly & Partlett 12th Edition* (Kindle Location 3880). Aspen Publishers (Wolters Kluwer Legal). Kindle Edition. Emanuel, Steven L. (2011-04-05). *Emanuel Law Outlines: Torts Keyed to Prosser Wade Schwartz Kelly & Partlett 12th Edition* (Kindle Locations 3879-3880). Aspen Publishers (Wolters Kluwer Legal). Kindle Edition. Emanuel, Steven L. (2011-04-05). *Emanuel Law Outlines: Torts Keyed to Prosser Wade Schwartz Kelly & Partlett 12th Edition* (Kindle Locations 3868-3869). Aspen Publishers (Wolters Kluwer Legal).

Kindle Edition. Emanuel, Steven L. (2011-04-05). Emanuel Law Outlines: Torts Keyed to Prosser Wade Schwartz Kelly & Partlett 12th Edition (Kindle Locations 4281-4284). Aspen Publishers (Wolters Kluwer Legal). Kindle Edition. Emanuel, Steven L. (2011-04-05). Emanuel Law Outlines: Torts Keyed to Prosser Wade Schwartz Kelly & Partlett 12th Edition (Kindle Locations 4284-4287). Aspen Publishers (Wolters Kluwer Legal). Kindle Edition. Emanuel, Steven L. (2011-04-05). Emanuel Law Outlines: Torts Keyed to Prosser Wade Schwartz Kelly & Partlett 12th Edition (Kindle Locations 3838-3839). Aspen Publishers (Wolters Kluwer Legal). Kindle Edition. Emanuel, Steven L. (2011-04-05). Emanuel Law Outlines: Torts Keyed to Prosser Wade Schwartz Kelly & Partlett 12th Edition (Kindle Locations 3791-3793). Aspen Publishers (Wolters Kluwer Legal). Kindle Edition.

9. Wikipedia

Appendix A Contracts and Other Evidence

C:\Users\fisherc3\Downloads\Purchase and Buy Sell Agreement (00247775).PDF

AGREEMENT

THIS AGREEMENT (the "Agreement"), is entered into as of the ____ day of July, 2012, (the "Effective Date") by and between **Cynthia Fisher**, a North Carolina resident, ("Buyer"), **Choice Med, Inc.**, a North Carolina corporation formerly known as Whaley Communications, LLC, ("Seller"), **Fisher RX Direct, LLC**, a North Carolina limited liability company, (the "Company"), **South Post, LLC**, a North Carolina limited liability company, ("Landlord"), **John & Harriett Whaley**, residents of North Carolina and **Carl Whaley**, a resident of North Carolina (collectively the "Parties").

W I T N E S S E T H:

WHEREAS, prior to May, 20, 2009, Buyer owned one hundred percent (100%) of the equity interests in the Company; and

WHEREAS, on May 20, 2009, Buyer agreed to convey to Seller membership interests in the Company as consideration for John & Harriett Whaley committing to loan the Company three hundred thousand dollars ($300,000.00); and

WHEREAS, as part of the sale that occurred on May 20, 2009, Carl Whaley was named as co-manager of the Company along with its existing manager, Buyer; and

WHEREAS, Carl Whaley has actively managed the Company on a day-to-day basis since the summer of 2011 and is owed by the Company eighty-five thousand dollars ($85,000.00) for his services; and

WHEREAS, the Company is in default of its financial obligations to John Whaley & Harriett Whaley and also to Carl Whaley; and

WHEREAS, at all times relevant to this Agreement, the Company has occupied certain premises owned by Landlord and continues to occupy said premises under a month-to-month lease; and

WHEREAS, the parties are desirous of the Seller selling back to Buyer the membership interest it owns in the Company.

NOW, THEREFORE, in consideration of the foregoing, the Parties agree as follows:

1. **Recitals.** The recitals contained above are true and incorporated herein as terms of this Agreement.

2. **Purchase & Sale.** The Seller hereby conveys to Buyer all right, title and interest it has in the Company.

3. **Acknowledgement of Debt.** The Parties hereby acknowledge that the Company is indebted to John & Harriett Whaley in the principal sum of three hundred thousand dollars ($300,000.00) and to Carl Whaley in the principal sum of eighty-five thousand dollars ($85,000.00).

4. **Modification of Terms of Debt.** In consideration of forbearance on the part of Carl Whaley and John & Harriett Whaley from exercising all remedies available to them for various defaults under the terms of the indebtedness, the Parties agree that the terms of the Company's indebtedness to the above-named individuals be modified to the following:

   a. Principal and interest due monthly
   b. Annual interest rate of seven percent (7%)
   c. Payments amortized over twelve (12) years such that the following monthly payments will be due:
      i. $3,085.14 to John & Harriett Whaley
      ii. $874.12 to Carl Whaley

d. A balloon payment of all principal and interest outstanding at the time shall be due five (5) years from the date of this agreement

e. Any existing collateral pledged under the prior terms of the loan shall remain as collateral under the modified terms

5. **Lease.** The Company agrees that the monthly periodic payment for its tenancy at 1157 East Marion Street, Suite 1, Shelby, NC shall be two thousand dollars ($2,000.00) per month to Landlord. Additionally, said tenancy shall be "triple net" with responsibility for a pro rata portion of ad valorem real estate taxes and insurance for the property and for all repairs associated with the portion of the property occupied by Company to be borne by the Company. Said repairs that are the responsibility of the Company include heating and air conditioning repair and replacement.

6. **Guaranty.** Buyer hereby agrees to personally guarantee all obligations of the Company currently due or due in the future to John & Harriett Whaley, Carl Whaley and Landlord.

7. **Confession of Judgment.** Company and Buyer will execute, simultaneous herewith, a confession of judgment for the sums owed by the Company and guaranteed by Buyer described hereinabove. Said confession of judgment shall not be filed with the Clerk of Court of Cleveland County for so long as payments are being made on the indebtedness according to the modified terms outlined above. The confession of judgment may be filed with the Clerk of Court for Cleveland County if a scheduled payment is not received on the indebtedness within ten (10) days after it is due.

8. **Release.** Buyer and Company ("Releasing Parties") hereby waive any all claims they may have against

Seller, Landlord, John & Harriet Whaley and Carl Whaley, their executors, heirs and assigns, whether said claims be known or unknown, accrued or un-accrued. Specifically, but not limited hereto, this waiver is meant to ratify any action taken by Carl Whaley while a Manager of the Company and absolve Carl Whaley from any liability to the Releasing Parties for said actions.

9.   **Completeness/Modification.**   This Agreement contains all terms of the arrangement between the Parties regarding the above-described investment and may not be amended except in writing signed by the Parties.

   IN WITNESS WHEREOF, the Parties have executed this Agreement as of the day and year first above written.

_____

Cynthia Fisher, **Buyer**

_____

Fisher RX Direct, LLC by Cynthia Fisher, Manager, **Company**

_____

Choice Med, Inc. by Carl Whaley, President, **Seller**

_____

South Post, LLC, by Carl Whaley, Manager, **Landlord**

_____

John Whaley, individually

Harriett Whaley, individually

Carl Whaley, individually

C:\Users\fisherc3\Downloads\CreationFiling C200724200416 9ffbe68d5bc94447976939a3c3 639d47.pdf

C:\Users\fisherc3\Downloads\DestructionFilin g C201314305052 b574a8758aec47ad96cfab2 9d2f1d815.pdf

C:\Users\fisherc3\Downloads\NorkusThomas0 8600.pdf

C:\Users\fisherc3\Desktop\Fisher Rx Direct\whaley police report - Copy.pdf

C:\Users\fisherc3\Desktop\Fisher Rx Direct\whaley police report2.pdf

C:\Users\fisherc3\Desktop\Fisher Rx Direct\whaley police report3.pdf

Appendix B Court Papers concerning Cynthia Fisher v. Whaley Communications (Med Choice Inc., John Whaley, Carl Whaley, and Alliance

Bank & Trust)(Superior Court Division: Cleveland County, Shelby NC) (13-CVS-579)

Victim Impact Statement

My name is Cynthia Fisher and I was 50 percent owner of Fisher Rx Direct when it was open. The following people and businesses were instrumental in helping Carl, John, and Harriet Whaley destroy Fisher Rx Direct and help the Whaleys embezzle over $100,000 from me.

Harriet Whaley – She was part owner of Fisher Rx Direct with her son Carl Whaley.
Carl Whaley – He was part owner of Fisher Rx Direct with is mother Harriet Whaley. Harriet and Carl Whaley owned 50 percent of Fisher Rx Direct.
John Whaley – he controlled Harriet and Carl Whaley and Shelia Cooper. He was and still is on the Board of Directors of Alliance Bank and Trust.
Shelia Cooper – was fired by me for refusing a direct order from me. I consider her an accomplice of the Whaleys.
Alliance Bank and Trust – held the Fisher Rx Direct bank account. The bank took me off the Fisher Rx Direct bank account without my permission because John and Carl Whaley told them to.

Community Pharmacy – they bought the patient files and other assets of Fisher Rx Direct without Cynthia Fisher's permission. Community Pharmacy bought stolen property because John, Carl, and Harriet Whaley owned 50 percent of Fisher Rx Direct but not 100 percent. I have given the District Attorney copies of everything and let him know the civil complaints files in this case. The civil complaints the criminal complaint involves 13-CVS-579 and 15-CVS-1141.

I lost my business, my house, and was forced into bankruptcy because of the actions of Carl Whaley, Harriet Whaley, John Whaley, Shelia Cooper. Alliance Bank and Trust, and Community Pharmacy. The crimes of the people and businesses just listed are felony embezzlement, felony larceny, felony coercion, and felony conspiracy.

I do not know what Harriet Whaley knew but her signature is on all the paperwork. I do know that John Whaley controls his entire family.

I have a civil complaint against Community Pharmacy and I only filed a civil complaint to get a copy of the check that Community Pharmacy wrote Carl and John Whaley for the Fisher Rx Direct patient files and other assets. I was sent a set of Admission questions by Community Pharmacy and I answered those questions to the best of my knowledge because the Whaleys did not allow me to have access to Fisher Rx Direct after they illegally kept me out of my pharmacy. If Community Pharmacy had given me the documents I asked for, I would have withdrawn the civil complaint.

I think the District Attorney might want to investigate and find out who is paying Wesley Deaton. I think John Whaley might be paying Wesley Deaton for Community Pharmacy. If he is, I feel that is further proof of a conspiracy between Community Pharmacy and the Whaleys. This is just a gut feeling on my part because I know how John Whaley operates. I have filed a complaint with the Judge concerning the way Wesley Deaton is treating me. The reason I think John Whaley is controlling Wesley Deaton behind the scenes is because the actions of Wesley Deaton is coming across to me as trying to bully me. In my opinion, John Whaley is a bully and he has made a habit of bullying people his whole life. And I would not let him bully me.

I have reopened my Bankruptcy thru my Bankruptcy Attorney Bill Gardner, because the complaint against Community Pharmacy is considered an asset of my Bankrupt estate and the counterclaim filed against me is considered a creditor of my Bankrupt estate.

I do not know what is going to happen with this investigation and I know that is up to the District Attorney and the courts. I do hope I can at least get restitution because of what has happened to me. I have written proof of how much it cost me to file bankruptcy. However, I have no clue how much Community Pharmacy paid John Whaley and Carl Whaley for patient files and other assets. I was never give a copy of the check and the Whaleys illegally kept me out of my pharmacy and would not take any of my phone calls. The Whaleys also never let recover my personal belongings from Fisher Rx Direct. However, I am praying that the District Attorney is able to obtain copies of the written checks to Carl and John Whaley for the patient files and assets. I was supposed to receive half of whatever the Whaleys sold the patient files and other assets of Fisher Rx Direct for. I had no choice but to declare bankruptcy and let them settle it civilly because I had no money to hire a law firm. There were plenty of large law firms interested but they wanted a large retainer and I did not have the money. So I did the only thing I could and that was to let the bankruptcy court handle it and I have. I was trying to get a copy of the checks mentioned above thru the civil process but it is not working, so far. I will have no problem testifying before a grand jury if I need to.

John Whaley is on the Board of Directors of Alliance Bank & Trust and he used his position on the Board to have Alliance Bank & Trust to keep me out of the business bank account and they would not allow back on the Fisher Rx Direct bank account unless I signed a buyout agreement that was extremely unfair. I think the District Attorney can go thru Alliance Bank & Trust to get copies of the checks mentioned above. I think each and every bank account of the Whaleys need to be subpoenaed. By the way, I am just making educated guesses on how copies of the checks can be obtained. Considering the fact that the Whaleys do not want to show me how much was paid to them for the sale of Fisher Rx Direct patient files and assets, I really do want to know. I still think it might have been $300,000.00. If it was $300,000, I am praying that I am allowed restitution of $150,000 plus court cost and attorney fees that I have had to pay out because of all the criminal actions committed against me. I think every criminal act committed against me comes under felonies and there are no statute of limitation on felonies in NC.

Cynthia Fisher v. Whaley Communications

Part 1
Issue: Tort of Conversion

Rule: The tort of conversion occurs when the defendant so substantially interferes with the plaintiff's possession or ownership of property that it is fair to require the defendant to pay the property's full value. See Rest. 2d §222A.
Ignorance of the law no excuse: Similarly, it is irrelevant that the defendant did not know that the action would constitute a tort or a crime. Thus in the law of intentional torts, "ignorance of the law is no excuse."
The intentional tortfeasor will be liable for virtually every result stemming directly or even somewhat indirectly from his conduct, however unlikely it might have seemed at the time of his act that this result would follow. Rest. 2d, §435B.

Analysis: Cynthia Fisher is 50 percent owner of Fisher Rx Direct and Whaley Communications is 50 percent owner of Fisher Rx Direct. Carl Whaley and John Whaley are head of Whaley Communications. Carl and John Whaley did not act in good faith. Carl and John Whaley completely destroyed Fisher Rx Direct while under their control which substantially interferes with Ms. Fisher's fifty percent ownership of Fisher Rx Direct. John and Carl Whaley did this out of complete spite because Cynthia Fisher started taking steps to get her part of Fisher Rx Direct back and to hopefully regain full control. Ms. Fisher was willing to continue to be a partner or work out a buy back agreement that would be fair to both parties. The Whaleys (Whaley Communications) had already sold the patient files of Fisher Rx Direct to another pharmacy without her knowledge and consent, while trying to coerce Ms. Fisher into signing an agreement that was horrible and could have destroyed her. The harm done to Fisher Rx Direct was its complete destruction. The expense and inconvenience caused to Ms. Fisher was considerable. Carl and John Whaley had illegally taken Ms. Fisher's name off of the Fisher Rx Direct Bank account at Alliance Bank. John Whaley is on the Board of Directors of Alliance Bank. Carl and John Whaley have refused to let Ms. Fisher access to the Fisher Rx Direct account at Alliance Bank for several months and continues to do so. Ms. Marquez, the attorney of Ms. Fisher, has contacted Mr. Farmer, the attorney for Carl Whaley, on several occasions concerning all these matters. The amount that Fisher Rx Direct received from other pharmacy for patient files is in question, because that information is being refused to us. Carl and John Whaley refused to pay for Ms. Fisher's attorney even after they were told that Fisher Rx Direct had to pay for Ms. Fisher's attorney, and they refused to pay checks written on the Fisher Rx Direct account, even after they were told they had to. The checks written by Ms. Fisher, for monthly expenses for Ms. Fisher never exceeded what she was owed in salary.

Conclusion: The Whaleys have no defenses because of what they tried to do to Ms. Fisher. Carl Whaley and John Whaley sold patient files and closed Fisher Rx Direct without Ms. Fisher's knowledge or consent.

Emanuel, Steven L. (2011-04-05). Emanuel Law Outlines: Torts Keyed to Prosser Wade Schwartz Kelly & Partlett 12th Edition (Kindle Locations 4928-4930). Aspen Publishers (Wolters Kluwer Legal). Kindle Edition.

Part 2:

Issue: Interference with existing contracts

Rule: the plaintiff loses the benefits of existing contracts.

Ignorance of the law no excuse: Similarly, it is irrelevant that the defendant did not know that the action would constitute a tort or a crime. Thus in the law of intentional torts, "ignorance of the law is no excuse."

The intentional tortfeasor will be liable for virtually every result stemming directly or even somewhat indirectly from his conduct, however unlikely it might have seemed at the time of his act that this result would follow. Rest. 2d, §435B.

Analysis: The pharmacy lost several patients because Ms. Fisher was not allowed back into her pharmacy. The patients stated they would come back when Ms. Fisher came back. Furthermore, Fisher Rx Direct was a back-up pharmacy for Hospice, as well as several nursing homes and assisted living centers. Fisher Rx Direct lost these contracts when Carl and John Whaley destroyed the pharmacy.

Conclusion: Whaley Communications owes Ms. Fisher compensatory damages for interference with prospective contracts.
Part 3:

Issue: Interference with Prospective Advantage

Rule: the plaintiff loses not the benefits of an existing contract, but simply the benefits of prospective, potential, contracts or other relationships.
Ignorance of the law no excuse: Similarly, it is irrelevant that the defendant did not know that the action would constitute a tort or a crime. Thus in the law of intentional torts, "ignorance of the law is no excuse."
The intentional tortfeasor will be liable for virtually every result stemming directly or even somewhat indirectly from his conduct, however unlikely it might have seemed at the time of his act that this result would follow. Rest. 2d, §435B.

Analysis: Ms. Fisher had been getting more customers for the business while she was trying to get control back of Fisher Rx Direct. These prospective patients were just waiting for her to get back to Fisher Rx Direct. Also, Ms. Fisher was hoping to work out something with the City of Shelby when she found out they needed a pharmacy to work with them on the city employees being able to afford their medication. The City of Shelby needs a good prescription plan. By Carl and John Whaley destroying the pharmacy, they put the brakes on that potential contract.

Conclusion: Whaley Communications owes Ms. Fisher compensation for interference with prospective contracts.

Emanuel, Steven L. (2011-04-05). Emanuel Law Outlines: Torts Keyed to Prosser Wade Schwartz Kelly & Partlett 12th Edition (Kindle Locations 17533-17534). Aspen Publishers (Wolters Kluwer Legal). Kindle Edition.

Part 4:
Issue: Defamation of Character

Rule: To be defamatory, a statement must have a tendency to harm the reputation of the plaintiff. Rest. 2d, §559. injured: For the statement to be defamatory, it is not necessary that it have actually injured the plaintiff's reputation; it must simply be the case that, if it had been believed, it would have had this effect. Thus even if the defendant can show that everyone who heard the statement believed that it was false, this will not prevent the statement from being defamatory. The defamatory statement must have an element of disgrace, the group the statement is communicated to must be respectable, and the statement must have a defamatory meaning. Libel is defamation in written form and slander is defamation in oral form or if there is special harm involved. Cases where no special harm necessary ("slander per se"): There are four kinds of utterances which, even though they are slander rather than libel, require no showing of special harm. These categories derive from a variety of historical factors, but their common element is that they are by their very nature especially likely to cause pecuniary harm. Such slander is generally called "slander per se." See P&K, p. 788-93. The categories are as follows: a. Crime: Statements imputing criminal behavior to the plaintiff. However, an accusation of a minor crime (e.g., a parking ticket) is not generally enough. The Restatement requires that the conduct imputed to the plaintiff either be "punishable by imprisonment" or "regarded by public opinion as involving moral turpitude". Rest. 2d, §571. The defamatory statement must be seen or heard by someone other than plaintiff.

Ignorance of the law no excuse: Similarly, it is irrelevant that the defendant did not know that the action would constitute a tort or a crime. Thus in the law of intentional torts, "ignorance of the law is no excuse."

The intentional tortfeasor will be liable for virtually every result stemming directly or even somewhat indirectly from his conduct, however unlikely it might have seemed at the time of his act that this result would follow. Rest. 2d, §435B.

Analysis: Carl and John Whaley accused Ms. Fisher of forgery and fraud, with actual malice. Actual malice is when the defendant knew statement was false or recklessly disregarded the truth. Both Carl and John Whaley knew what they were accusing Ms. Fisher was false and they did care about the truth. The conduct imputed to Ms. Fisher could have been punishable by imprisonment. Carl and John Whaley told Alliance Bank that the checks Ms. Fisher wrote to pay her salary and bills was forgery and fraud even though Ms. Fisher has a legal right to write checks on the Fisher Rx Direct bank account at Alliance Bank because Ms. Fisher owns 50% of Fisher Rx Direct. The special harm caused to Ms. Fisher was that First National Bank closed her personal account because she was accused of forgery and fraud. She also had to pay fees on returned checks which Carl and John Whaley refused to pay even after they were told they had too. Forgery and fraud was written on the returned checks.

Conclusion: Whaley Communications owes Ms. Fisher compensatory and punitive damages for Defamation of Character.

Emanuel, Steven L. (2011-04-05). Emanuel Law Outlines: Torts Keyed to Prosser Wade Schwartz

Kelly & Partlett 12th Edition (Kindle Locations 16378-16385). Aspen Publishers (Wolters Kluwer Legal). Kindle Edition. Emanuel, Steven L. (2011-04-05). Emanuel Law Outlines: Torts Keyed to Prosser Wade Schwartz Kelly & Partlett 12th Edition (Kindle Locations 16167-16170). Aspen Publishers (Wolters Kluwer Legal). Kindle Edition. Emanuel, Steven L. (2011-04-05). Emanuel Law Outlines: Torts Keyed to Prosser Wade Schwartz Kelly & Partlett 12th Edition (Kindle Locations 16163-16164). Aspen Publishers (Wolters Kluwer Legal). Kindle Edition.

Part 5:

Issue: Malicious Prosecution

Rules: To make out a prima facie case of malicious prosecution, the plaintiff must prove the following elements: (1) that the defendant instituted criminal proceedings against him; (2) that these proceedings terminated in favor of the plaintiff (the accused); (3) that the defendant had no probable cause to institute the proceedings; and (4) that the defendant was motivated primarily by some purpose other than bringing an offender to justice. See Rest. 2d, §653; P&K, p. 871.

Initiating proceeding: The plaintiff must show that the defendant took an active part in instigating and encouraging the prosecution. For instance, if the defendant merely states what she believes to be the facts to the prosecutor, and leaves to the latter the decision whether to prosecute, this will probably not be "institution" of proceedings. But if the defendant has attempted to influence a district attorney to prosecute, or has lied so as to make prosecution more probable, this will be sufficient. See P&K, p. 872-73.

i.   Mistake of law: But a lay person's erroneous belief that certain conduct constitutes a crime is quite likely to be held to be unreasonable, if it is not arrived at after consultation with a lawyer or prosecutor. Once the defendant does receive assurances of her lawyer or the prosecutor that these facts constitute a crime, however, she has probable cause (assuming that she has made full disclosure of the facts known to her). See Rest. 2d, §662, Comment i and §666.

ii.   The intentional tortfeasor will be liable for virtually every result stemming directly or even somewhat indirectly from his conduct, however unlikely it might have seemed at the time of his act that this result would follow. Rest. 2d, §435B.

Emanuel, Steven L. (2011-04-05). Emanuel Law Outlines: Torts Keyed to Prosser Wade Schwartz Kelly & Partlett 12th Edition (Kindle Locations 17295-17298). Aspen Publishers (Wolters Kluwer Legal). Kindle Edition.
Emanuel, Steven L. (2011-04-05). Emanuel Law Outlines: Torts Keyed to Prosser Wade Schwartz Kelly & Partlett 12th Edition (Kindle Locations 17275-17279). Aspen Publishers (Wolters Kluwer Legal). Kindle Edition.

Analysis: From what Ms. Fisher understand John Whaley lied to the DA to try and get Ms. Fisher prosecuted for forgery or fraud. He told the DA that Ms. Fisher had no legal right to write checks on the Fisher Rx Direct business account because he had fired her. Neither John Whaley nor Carl Whaley had to legal right to fire Ms. Fisher because she is 50% owner of Fisher Rx Direct. Ms. Fisher did fire an employee for directly disobeying a direct order from Ms. Fisher and Ms. Fisher had the legal right to do that as 50% owner of Fisher Rx Direct. Carl Whaley admitted to the detective that came to Ms. Fisher's house that she was 50%

owner of Fisher Rx Direct. Ms. Fisher provided proof of 50% ownership to the detective and the warrant was dismissed by the DA. Ms. Fisher believes that Mr. John Whaley's actions were pure vindictiveness because she would not let him have total control of Fisher Rx Direct. Ms. Fisher was willing to still be partner or work out a fair buyout agreement, in which she could buy them out. Mr. John Whaley was not willing to do this. Mr. Carl Whaley might have felt the same way but Ms. Fisher does not think so, because he had told her himself personally he did not enjoy working in the pharmacy, he preferred working outside. Ms. Fisher does not think that neither Carl nor John Whaley consulted their attorney or the DA before sending back checks from the Fisher Rx Direct Alliance Bank Account accusing her of forgery/fraud. Ms. Fisher believes this because the checks were sent back after they cleared the bank. The checks Ms. Fisher wrote against the Alliance bank account was for bills and attorney fees because she was being refused her salary by Carl and John Whaley. They were trying to bankrupt her in order to take her business, so she could not hire an attorney. The DA stopped the proceedings as soon as Ms. Fisher proved that she was 50% owner of Fisher Rx Direct. According to the contract between Whaley Communications and Fisher Rx Direct (Dr. Cynthia A. Fisher), all attorney fees for each party are to be paid for by Fisher Rx Direct.

Conclusion: Ms. Fisher has an action against Whaley Communication for lost income as well as emotional and mental distress.

Emanuel, Steven L. (2011-04-05). Emanuel Law Outlines: Torts Keyed to Prosser Wade Schwartz Kelly & Partlett 12th Edition (Kindle Locations 17271-17275). Aspen Publishers (Wolters Kluwer Legal). Kindle Edition

Part 6:
Issue: Abuse of process

Rule: Abuse of process: Even if a criminal or civil proceeding is brought with probable cause, and for allowable motives, a person involved in it may use various litigation devices available to him during the course of it for improper purposes. If so, he will be liable for "abuse of process."
Ignorance of the law no excuse: Similarly, it is irrelevant that the defendant did not know that the action would constitute a tort or a crime. Thus in the law of intentional torts, "ignorance of the law is no excuse."
The intentional tortfeasor will be liable for virtually every result stemming directly or even somewhat

indirectly from his conduct, however unlikely it might have seemed at the time of his act that this result would follow. Rest. 2d, §435B.

Analysis: Mr. Carl Whaley and Mr. John Whaley had Alliance bank send back checks that Ms. Fisher wrote to pay bills and pay her attorney by telling the bank it was forgery/fraud. Mr. John Whaley is on the Board of Directors of Alliance and Ms. Fisher believes Mr. John Whaley was able to get this done without going thru proper channels because of his position on the Board of Directors at Alliance. Alliance refused to allow Ms. Fisher access to the Fisher Rx Direct bank account even after being told that Ms. Fisher had the legal right to have access to that account. Mr. John Whaley and Mr. Carl Whaley still refused to pay the checks even after they were told that Ms. Fisher had the legal right to write checks on the Fisher Rx Direct Alliance bank account.

Conclusion: Mr. John and Mr. Carl Whaley were being vindictive and malicious in their abuse of process. Ms. Fisher would like the bank to require that Mr. John Whaley step down from being on the Board of Directors of Alliance bank and should not be allowed to be on the Board of Directors of any bank again. Ms. Fisher might have actions against Alliance Bank because they allowed John and Carl

Whaley to take her off the bank account without checking with Ms. Fisher herself and she is the only one that should have had the authority to take herself off the Alliance Bank account. The DA has resolved everything in Ms. Fisher's favor.

Emanuel, Steven L. (2011-04-05). Emanuel Law Outlines: Torts Keyed to Prosser Wade Schwartz Kelly & Partlett 12th Edition (Kindle Locations 17361-17363). Aspen Publishers (Wolters Kluwer Legal). Kindle Edition.

Part 7
Issue: Intentional Infliction of Mental and Emotional Distress

Rule: Intentional or reckless infliction, by extreme and outrageous conduct, of severe emotional or mental distress, even in the absence of physical harm. Intent: In the intentional torts we have examined so far (battery, assault and false imprisonment), we have seen that the requisite intent may exist not only where the defendant desires to cause a certain result, but also where she knows with "substantial certainty" that the result will occur. In the case of infliction of mental distress, however, the necessary mental state is even broader—there are three possible mental states on D's part, any of which will qualify: [a] D desires to cause P emotional distress; [b] D knows with substantial certainty that P will suffer emotional distress; and [c] D recklessly disregards the high probability that emotional distress will occur.

Ignorance of the law no excuse: Similarly, it is irrelevant that the defendant did not know that the action would constitute a tort or a crime. Thus in the law of intentional torts, "ignorance of the law is no excuse."

Punitive damages: An intentional tort victim may recover punitive damages, if the defendant's conduct was outrageous or malicious. Rest. 2d, §908.

The intentional tortfeasor will be liable for virtually every result stemming directly or even somewhat indirectly from his conduct, however unlikely it might have seemed at the time of his act that this result would follow. Rest. 2d, §435B.

Analysis: Carl and John Whaley of Whaley Communications knew exactly what Ms. Fisher has gone thru this past year and they committed all of the torts discussed in this brief anyway. Ms. Fisher could not afford insurance because Carl and John Whaley refused to pay her even after they were told she had the legal right to get paid from Fisher Rx Direct. Carl and John Whaley refused to pay Kings Law Offices even after they were told they had to because of the buy/sell agreement between Ms. Fisher and Whaley Communications. Carl and John Whaley of Whaley Communications deliberately desired to cause Ms. Fisher emotional distress, knew with substantial certainty that Ms. Fisher would suffer emotional distress, and recklessly disregarded the high probability that emotional distress would occur. Each and every action of Carl and John Whaley was against Ms. Fisher was an intentional tort.

Conclusion: Ms. Fisher can collect punitive damages from Whaley Communications based on the intentional actions of Carl and John Whaley of Whaley Communications concerning the tort of intentional infliction of mental and emotional distress.

Emanuel, Steven L. (2011-04-05). Emanuel Law Outlines: Torts Keyed to Prosser Wade Schwartz Kelly & Partlett 12th Edition (Kindle Location 3880). Aspen Publishers (Wolters Kluwer Legal). Kindle Edition. Emanuel, Steven L. (2011-04-05). Emanuel Law Outlines: Torts Keyed to Prosser Wade Schwartz Kelly & Partlett 12th Edition (Kindle Locations 3879-3880). Aspen Publishers (Wolters Kluwer Legal). Kindle Edition. Emanuel, Steven L. (2011-04-05). Emanuel Law Outlines: Torts Keyed to Prosser Wade Schwartz Kelly &

Partlett 12th Edition (Kindle Locations 3868-3869). Aspen Publishers (Wolters Kluwer Legal). Kindle Edition. Emanuel, Steven L. (2011-04-05). Emanuel Law Outlines: Torts Keyed to Prosser Wade Schwartz Kelly & Partlett 12th Edition (Kindle Locations 4281-4284). Aspen Publishers (Wolters Kluwer Legal). Kindle Edition. Emanuel, Steven L. (2011-04-05). Emanuel Law Outlines: Torts Keyed to Prosser Wade Schwartz Kelly & Partlett 12th Edition (Kindle Locations 4284-4287). Aspen Publishers (Wolters Kluwer Legal). Kindle Edition. Emanuel, Steven L. (2011-04-05). Emanuel Law Outlines: Torts Keyed to Prosser Wade Schwartz Kelly & Partlett 12th Edition (Kindle Locations 3838-3839). Aspen Publishers (Wolters Kluwer Legal). Kindle Edition. Emanuel, Steven L. (2011-04-05). Emanuel Law Outlines: Torts Keyed to Prosser Wade Schwartz Kelly & Partlett 12th Edition (Kindle Locations 3791-3793). Aspen Publishers (Wolters Kluwer Legal). Kindle Edition.

Overall Conclusion: The only way the actions of Carl and John Whaley against Ms. Fisher can be described is atrocious. Ms. Fisher tried to work with both Carl and John Whaley to even buy back their part of the pharmacy from them. They tried to get Ms. Fisher to sign a horrible contract. Mr. Josh Farmer stated he did not draw up the contract. Ms.

Fisher believes John and Carl Whaley found a contract on the internet and tried to coerce Ms. Fisher into signing it. Ms. Fisher did refuse to sign said contract based on the advice of her attorney. Ms. Fisher and her attorney do have copies of said contract. There is also evidence that points to the diversion of funds from Fisher Rx Direct to Whaley Communications and/or John and Carl Whaley personally. Mr. John Whaley used his position on the Board of Directors of Alliance Bank to try and cause Ms. Fisher financial hardship, which further resulted in intentional infliction of mental and emotional distress. Ms. Fisher could have action against Alliance bank based on the action of Mr. John Whaley's abuse of his position on the Board of Directors. Ms. Fisher is owed compensatory and punitive damages from Whaley Communications because of the tort actions committed against her by Carl and John Whaley. Ms. Fisher might be owed compensatory and punitive damages from Alliance Bank & Trust based on John Whaley's abuse of his position on the Board of Directors of Alliance Bank and Trust. Carl and John Whaley do not have the defense of mistake of law because that is not a defense when intentional torts are committed. The intentional tortfeasor will be liable for virtually every result stemming directly or even somewhat indirectly from his conduct, however unlikely it might have seemed at the time of his act that this result would follow. The actions of John and Carl Whaley of Whaley Communications were intentional torts against Ms. Fisher.

Official Tort Complaint
Cynthia A. Fisher

v

Choice Med, INC (formerly Whaley Communications)
Carl Whaley
John Whaley
Alliance Bank & Trust

Ms. Fisher was part owner of Fisher Rx Direct until John Whaley and Carl Whaley converted it. Ms. Fisher is a pharmacist and graduated from Concord School of Law in June 2011. Ms. Fisher has a Doctorate of Pharmacy and an Executive Juris Doctor. My partner is Whaley Communications, now Choice Med, Inc. The name was changed in November 2011. The proof of this is on file at the Secretary of State.

1. **Choice Med Inc, and John and Carl Whaley and Alliance Bank & Trust committed the tort of conversion against Ms. Cynthia A. Fisher. A prima facie case of conversion occurs when the defendant so substantially interferes with the plaintiff's possession or ownership of property that it is fair to require the defendant to pay the**

**property's full value. See Rest. 2d §222A.
Substantial interference occurred when the
patient files were sold without her knowledge or
permission, closing the business, refusing to
return personal property, and missing funds.**

Cynthia Fisher is 50 percent owner of Fisher Rx Direct and
Whaley Communications is 50 percent owner of Fisher Rx
Direct. Carl Whaley and John Whaley are head of Whaley
Communications. Whaley Communications is now Choice
Med Inc. Carl and John Whaley did not act in good faith.
The funds that Carl Whaley and John Whaley bought their
50% ownership of Fisher Rx Direct, Ms Fisher put back
into the pharmacy and Carl and John Whaley refused to
put matching funds into Fisher Rx Direct. Honest
businessmen told me that when I put the proceeds of the
selling of fifty percent of Fisher Rx Direct back into the
business, that Carl and John Whaley was supposed to
match those funds because they were my equal partners.
Carl and John Whaley completely destroyed Fisher Rx
Direct while under their control which substantially
interferes with Ms. Fisher's fifty percent ownership of
Fisher Rx Direct. John and Carl Whaley did this out of
complete spite because Cynthia Fisher started taking steps
to get her part of Fisher Rx Direct back and to hopefully
regain full control. Ms. Fisher was willing to continue to
be a partner or work out a buy back agreement that would
be fair to both parties. John and Carl Whaley had already
sold the patient files of Fisher Rx Direct to another
pharmacy without her knowledge and consent, while
trying to coerce Ms. Fisher into signing an agreement that
was horrible and could have destroyed her. The harm done

to Fisher Rx Direct was its complete destruction. The expense and inconvenience caused to Ms. Fisher was considerable. Carl and John Whaley had illegally taken Ms. Fisher's name off of the Fisher Rx Direct Bank account at Alliance Bank & Trust. John Whaley is on the Board of Directors of Alliance Bank and used his position on the Board of Directors to have these illegal acts done. Carl and John Whaley have refused to let Ms. Fisher access to the Fisher Rx Direct account at Alliance Bank for several months and continues to do so. Ms. Marquez, the attorney of Ms. Fisher, has contacted Mr. Farmer, the attorney for Mr. Carl and John Whaley and Choice Med, Inc (formerly Whaley Communications), on several occasions concerning all these matters. The amount that Fisher Rx Direct received from other pharmacy for patient files is in question, because that information is being refused to us. Carl and John Whaley refused to pay for Ms. Fisher's attorney even after they were told that Fisher Rx Direct had to pay for Ms. Fisher's attorney, and they refused to pay checks written on the Fisher Rx Direct account, even after they were told they had to. The checks written by Ms. Fisher, for monthly expenses for Ms. Fisher never exceeded what she was owed in salary. John and Carl Whaley will contend that Ms. Fisher had complete control over all insurance proceeds, but she did not. Carl Whaley and John Whaley had access to funds for several months and these funds are missing, which included cash, credit card payments, all 3rd party insurance payments, and checks. Ms. Fisher was able to gain control of Central Pay and Medicaid payments for a month, and then Cardinal was able to gain control of Central Pay payments because Carl Whaley stopped paying the bill to them as well as several other bills. The funds received from the selling of the patient files is also missing. Ms. Fisher had no choice but to get control of some funds in order to pay her attorney and pay bills because of the actions of John and Carl Whaley. Mr. Carl and John Whaley tried to bankrupt Ms. Fisher, so she could not take them to court. Mr. Carl and John Whaley opened a new account for Fisher Rx Direct at Alliance Bank & Trust and shut down the old account for Fisher Rx Direct at Alliance Bank & Trust. Alliance Bank & Trust did not contact Ms. Fisher to get her permission for either of the preceding actions. Ms. Fisher is the only person on the Articles of Corporation and she is the only one allowed to open or close a bank account for Fisher Rx Direct. Choice Med Inc, Carl Whaley, John Whaley, and Alliance Bank & Trust should pay to Ms. Fisher, the full market value of Fisher Rx Direct because Whaley Communications (now Choice Med Inc) destroyed Fisher Rx Direct. This is just referring to the compensatory damages that should be given to Ms. Fisher. Ms. Fisher should also receive punitive damages from Choice Med Inc, Carl Whaley, John Whaley, and Alliance Bank & Trust because of the actions of John Whaley, Carl Whaley, and Alliance Bank & Trust taken against her personally. Carl and John Whaley have a pattern of this type of behavior. The intent of John Whaley and Carl Whaley all along was to try to steal Fisher Rx Direct from Cynthia A. Fisher. The missing funds occurred because Alliance Bank & Trust allowed John and Carl Whaley access and did not verify anything with Ms. Fisher.

2. **Choice Med Inc, and John and Carl Whaley committed the tort of interference of existing contracts against Ms. Cynthia A. Fisher. A prima**

facie case exists for the tort of interference with existing contracts occurs when the plaintiff loses the benefits of existing contracts. The selling of the patient files was interference with existing contracts.

Furthermore, Fisher Rx Direct was a back-up pharmacy for Hospice, as well as several nursing homes and assisted living centers. Fisher Rx Direct lost these contracts when Carl and John Whaley destroyed the pharmacy. Selling of current patient files is further evidence of interference of existing contracts. Choice Med Inc, Carl Whaley, and John Whaley owe Ms. Fisher compensatory damages for interference with existing contracts.

3. **Choice Med Inc, and John and Carl Whaley committed the tort of interference of prospective advantage against Ms. Cynthia A. Fisher. A prima facie case exists for the tort of interference of prospective contracts occurwhen the plaintiff loses not the benefits of an existing contract, but simply the benefits of prospective, potential contracts or other relationships. The destruction of Fisher Rx Direct interfered with the benefits of prospective, potential contracts or other relationships.**

Ms. Fisher had been getting more customers for the business while she was trying to get control back of Fisher Rx Direct. Also, Ms. Fisher was hoping to work out something with the City of Shelby when she found out they needed a pharmacy to work with them, so the city employees would be able to afford their medication. The City of Shelby needs a good prescription plan. By Carl and John Whaley destroying the pharmacy, they put the brakes on that potential contract. Choice Med, Inc, Carl Whaley, and John Whaley owe Ms. Fisher compensation for interference with prospective contracts.

4. **Choice Med Inc, and Alliance Bank & Trust and John Whaley and Carl Whaley committed the tort of malicious prosecution against Ms. Cynthia A. Fisher. To make out a prima facie case of malicious prosecution, the plaintiff must prove the following elements: (1) that the defendant instituted criminal proceedings against him; (2) that these proceedings terminated in favor of the plaintiff (the accused); (3) that the defendant had no probable cause to institute the proceedings; and (4) that the defendant was motivated primarily by some purpose other than bringing an offender to justice. See Rest. 2d, §653; P&K. John and Carl Whaley instituted criminal proceedings against Ms. Fisher and the proceedings terminated in my favor when the DA dismissed the case, John and Carl Whaley had no probable cause to institute the proceedings against Ms. Fisher. John and Carl Whaley was motivated by vindictiveness and greed, which is motivation by some other purpose than bringing an offender to justice.**

From what Ms. Fisher understands John Whaley lied to the DA to try and get Ms. Fisher prosecuted for forgery or fraud. He told the DA that Ms. Fisher had no legal right to write checks on the Fisher Rx Direct business account because he had fired her. Neither John Whaley nor Carl Whaley had to legal right to fire Ms. Fisher because she is 50% owner of Fisher Rx Direct. Ms. Fisher did fire an employee for directly disobeying a direct order from Ms. Fisher and Ms. Fisher had the legal right to do that as 50% owner of Fisher Rx Direct. Carl Whaley admitted to the detective that came to Ms. Fisher's house that she was 50% owner of Fisher Rx Direct. Ms. Fisher provided proof of 50% ownership to the detective and the warrant was dismissed by the DA. Ms. Fisher believes that Mr. John and Carl Whaley's actions were pure vindictiveness because she would not let him have total control of Fisher Rx Direct. Ms. Fisher was willing to still be a partner or work out a fair buyout agreement, in which she could buy them out. Mr. John Whaley was not willing to do this. Mr. Carl Whaley might have felt the same way but Ms. Fisher does not think so, because he had told her himself personally he did not enjoy working in the pharmacy, he preferred working outside. Ms. Fisher does not think that neither Carl nor John Whaley consulted their attorney or the DA before sending back checks from the Fisher Rx Direct Alliance Bank Account accusing her of forgery/fraud. Ms. Fisher believes this because the checks were sent back after they cleared the bank. The checks Ms. Fisher wrote against the Alliance bank account was for bills and attorney fees because she was being refused her salary by Carl and John Whaley. They were trying to bankrupt her in order to take her business, so she could not hire an attorney and take them to court. The DA stopped the proceedings as soon as Ms. Fisher proved that she was 50% owner of Fisher Rx Direct. According to the contract between Whaley Communications and Fisher Rx Direct (Dr. Cynthia A. Fisher), all attorney fees for each party are to be paid for by Fisher Rx Direct. Choice Med Inc, Carl Whaley, John Whaley, and Alliance Bank & Trust owe Ms. Fisher compensatory damages and punitive damages because of the actions taken against her personally.

5. **Choice Med, Inc, Mr. Carl Whaley, Mr. John Whaley, and Alliance Bank & Trust committed the tort of abuse of process against Ms. Cynthia A. Fisher. A prima facie case exists for abuse of process because John Whaley and Carl Whaley instituted criminal proceedings against Ms. Fisher without probable cause.**

Mr. Carl Whaley and Mr. John Whaley had Alliance bank send back checks that Ms. Fisher wrote to pay bills and pay her attorney by telling the bank it was forgery/fraud. Mr. John Whaley is on the Board of Directors of Alliance and Ms. Fisher believes Mr. John Whaley was able to get this done without going thru proper channels because of his position on the Board of Directors at Alliance. Alliance refused to allow Ms. Fisher access to the Fisher Rx Direct bank account even after being told that Ms. Fisher had the legal right to have access to that account. Mr. John Whaley and Mr. Carl Whaley still refused to pay the checks even after they were told that Ms. Fisher had the legal right to write checks on the Fisher Rx Direct Alliance bank account(s). Mr. John and Mr. Carl Whaley were being vindictive and malicious in their abuse of process. Ms. Fisher might have actions against Alliance Bank because they allowed John and Carl Whaley to take her off the bank account without checking with Ms. Fisher herself and she is the only one that should have had the authority to take herself off the Alliance Bank account. The DA has resolved everything in Ms. Fisher's favor. Choice Med Inc, Carl Whaley, John Whaley, and Alliance Bank & Trust owe Ms. Fisher compensatory damages and punitive damages because of the tort of abuse of process.

6. **Choice Med Inc, Mr. Carl Whaley, Mr. John Whaley, and Alliance Bank &Trust committed the tort of defamation of character against Ms. Cynthia A. Fisher. A prima facie case for the tort of defamation of character exists when a statement must have a tendency to harm the reputation of the plaintiff. Rest. 2d, §559. For the statement to be defamatory it is not necessary that it have actually injured the plaintiff's reputation. The defamatory statement must have an element of disgrace, the group the statement is communicated to must be respectable, and the statement must have a defamatory meaning. Libel is defamation in written form and slander is defamation in oral form or if there is special harm involved. Cases where no special harm necessary ("slander per se"): There are four kinds of utterances which, even though they are slander rather than libel, require no showing of**

special harm. These categories derive from a variety of historical factors, but their common element is that they are by their very nature especially likely to cause pecuniary harm. Such slander is generally called "slander per se." See P&K, p. 788-93. The categories are as follows: a. Crime: Statements imputing criminal behavior to the plaintiff. However, an accusation of a minor crime (e.g., a parking ticket) is not generally enough. The Restatement requires that the conduct imputed to the plaintiff either be "punishable by imprisonment" or "regarded by public opinion as involving moral turpitude". Rest. 2d, §571. The defamatory statement must be seen or heard by someone other than plaintiff. John and Carl Whaley bringing criminal proceedings against plaintiff prove the prima facie case of slander per se. Some of the third parties the defamation was communicated to were: First National Bank, David Fisher, Kings Law Offices etc... Forgery/fraud was written by Alliance Bank & Trust on each returned check. The written element for libel is satisfied.

Carl and John Whaley accused Ms. Fisher of forgery and fraud, with actual malice. Actual malice is when the defendant knew statement was false or recklessly disregarded the truth. Both Carl and John Whaley knew what they were accusing Ms. Fisher of was false and they did not care about the truth. The conduct imputed to Ms.

Fisher could have been punishable by imprisonment. Carl and John Whaley told Alliance Bank that the checks Ms. Fisher wrote to pay her salary and bills was forgery and fraud even though Ms. Fisher has a legal right to write checks on the Fisher Rx Direct bank account at Alliance Bank because Ms. Fisher owns 50% of Fisher Rx Direct. The special harm caused to Ms. Fisher was that First National Bank closed her personal account because she was accused of forgery and fraud. She also had to pay fees on returned checks which Carl and John Whaley refused to pay even after they were told they had too. Forgery and fraud was written on the returned checks. John Whaley, Carl Whaley, Choice Med Inc, and Alliance Bank & Trust committed libel and slander per se. Slander per se is an issue because John Whaley, Carl Whaley, Choice Med Inc, and Alliance Bank & Trust accused me of a crime. The DA dismissed the warrant. Choice Med Inc, Carl Whaley, John Whaley, and Alliance Bank & Trust owe Ms. Fisher compensatory damages and punitive damages because of defamation of character.

7. **Choice Med Inc, Carl Whaley and John Whaley committed the tort of intentional misrepresentation. A prima facie case of misrepresentation exists when there is a misrepresentation by the defendant. The defendant must have a culpable state of mind, the defendant must have the intent to induce the plaintiff's reliance on the misrepresentation, and cause damage to the plaintiff. Carl Whaley made a misrepresentation to Ms. Fisher, had a culpable state of mind, had the intent to induce Ms.**

Fisher's reliance on the misrepresentation and caused damage to Ms. Fisher because he sold patient files and closed Fisher Rx Direct.

Carl Whaley tried to coerce Ms. Fisher into signing an unconscionable contract in order to buy back the business. An agreement that is grossly unjust, unfair, or dishonest may be deemed an unconscionable contract. Determining whether or not an agreement is unconscionable usually raises questions of competency, fairness, and honesty. If it is found that these things have been manipulated in such a way that an agreement is shocking to the conscience of a normal person, a court will not allow the contract to be enforced. Ms. Fisher and her attorney, Ms. Marquez have a copy of said contract and will be submitting the contract as evidence against Mr. Carl Whaley, Mr. John Whaley, and Choice Med Inc. The contract will provide proof of the value of the pharmacy. Furthermore, Ms. Fisher discovered after talking to honest business people that she is owed further compensation because of putting the funds received from the buy-sell agreement back into the business. Choice Med Inc, Carl Whaley, and John Whaley owe compensation to Fisher Rx Direct because they were supposed to match any funds Ms. Cynthia A. Fisher put back into the business. Instead of putting the funds into her pocket, Ms. Fisher put the funds back into Fisher Rx Direct and Choice Med Inc, Carl Whaley, and John Whaley did not put anymore funds into Fisher Rx Direct. The final payment for fifty percent of Fisher Rx Direct was made in January 2010. Ms. Fisher later found out that the funds from the buy-sell agreement should have went into her pocket and she and Carl Whaley, and John Whaley were supposed to put matching funds back into Fisher Rx

Direct because they were now fifty percent partners. I have business men willing to testify to this. Choice Med Inc, Carl Whaley, and John Whaley, owe Ms. Fisher compensation because of the tort of misrepresentation. They owe the compensation to Ms. Fisher because they destroyed Fisher Rx Direct.

8. **Choice Med Inc, Carl Whaley, John Whaley, and Alliance Bank & Trust committed the tort of intentional infliction of mental and emotional distress against Ms. Cynthia A. Fisher. A prima facie case for the intentional tort of intentional infliction of mental or emotional distress occurs when intentional or reckless inflictions, by extreme and outrageous conduct, of severe emotional or mental distress, even in the absence of physical harm. In the case of intentional infliction of mental distress and emotional distress, there are three possible mental states on defendant's part, any of which will qualify: [a] Defendant desires to cause Plaintiff emotional distress; [b] Defendant knows with substantial certainty that Plaintiff will suffer emotional distress; and [c] Defendant recklessly disregards the high probability that emotional distress will occur.**

Mr. Carl Whaley and Mr. John Whaley knew exactly what Ms. Fisher has gone thru this past year and they committed all of the torts discussed in this complaint anyway. Ms. Fisher could not afford insurance because Carl Whaley and

John Whaley refused to pay her even after they were told she had the legal right to get paid from Fisher Rx Direct. Carl and John Whaley refused to pay Kings Law Offices even after they were told they had to because of the buy/sell agreement between Ms. Fisher and Whaley Communications (now Choice Med, Inc). Carl and John Whaley deliberately desired to cause Ms. Fisher emotional distress, knew with substantial certainty that Ms. Fisher would suffer emotional distress, and recklessly disregarded the high probability that emotional distress would occur. Each and every action of Carl and John Whaley taken against Ms. Fisher was an intentional tort. Choice Med Inc, Carl Whaley, John Whaley, and Alliance Bank & Trust owe Ms. Fisher punitive damages because of intentional infliction of mental and emotional distress.

Ignorance of the law no excuse: Similarly, it is irrelevant that the defendant did not know that the action would constitute a tort or a crime. Thus in the law of intentional torts, "ignorance of the law is no excuse."

Punitive damages: An intentional tort victim may recover punitive damages, if the defendant's conduct was outrageous or malicious. Rest. 2d, §908.

The intentional tortfeasor will be liable for virtually every result stemming directly or even somewhat indirectly from his conduct, however unlikely it might have seemed at the time of his act that this result would follow. Rest. 2d, §435B.

The actions of Carl Whaley and John Whaley were outrageous and malicious which satisfies the requirement for punitive damages. Ms. Fisher is seeking compensation damages for the conversion and destruction of Fisher Rx Direct. Ms. Fisher is seeking

compensatory damages and punitive damages because of actions committed against her personally and against Fisher Rx Direct. Ms. Fisher is seeking compensatory damages and punitive damages from Mr. John Whaley, Mr. Carl Whaley, Alliance Bank & Trust, and Choice Med Inc, (formerly Whaley Communications). Ms. Fisher is seeking money for claim of relief in the form of compensation damages in the amount of $1,000,000 and punitive damages in the amount of $3,000,000. Ms. Fisher is also seeking the return of any personal property that Carl Whaley, John Whaley or Choice Med Inc, still has in their possession. Choice Med, Inc (formerly Whaley Communications) is/was Ms. Fisher's business partner. Carl Whaley is the owner and president of Choice Med Inc. John Whaley is the secretary of Choice Med, Inc. John Whaley is on the Board of Directors of Alliance Bank & Trust and he used his position to illegally take over the bank account and open a new account for Fisher Rx Direct and to allow Carl Whaley and John Whaley to convert funds.

Memorandum Of Law regarding Cynthia Ann Fisher (plaintiff) against Carl Whaley, John Whaley, Alliance Bank & Trust, and Choice Med INC. (defendants)

Case #: 13 CVS 579

According to the North Carolina General Statute Section 75-1.1, all defendants have each violated this statute multiple times. An action brought under NC Gen Stat Sec. 75-1.1 exists independently and is usually tacked on common law causes of actions. There were several common law causes of action committed against Ms. Fisher by the defendants in this complaint. To determine if a prima facie case exists, there is a three prong test. The first part of the test is to determine if commerce was affected. Second, it is determined if a practice is unfair or deceptive, but it does not have to be both. Third and final, the unfair and/or deceptive acts must be the proximate cause of the injury to the plaintiff. A practice is unfair when it offends established public policy or when the act or practice is "immoral, unethical, oppressive, unscrupulous, or substantially injurious to consumers. A party is guilty of an unfair act or practice when it engages in conduct which amounts to an inequitable assertion of its power or position. A claimant must prove that a defendant's unfair or deceptive acts were the cause of the injuries the claimant incurred. Proof of actual injuries can include: loss of the use of specific and unique property, the loss of any appreciated value of property, and other elements of damage shown by plaintiff's evidence. Fisher Rx Direct was a commercial enterprise, it was a pharmacy and it was there for private consumers and for health care facilities. Furthermore, Fisher Rx Direct had expanding pharmacy business beyond Cleveland County into the surrounding cities and counties and included delivery of medications to paying accounts, establishing a growing customer base, and building goodwill through services provided. Ms. Fisher, through Fisher Rx Direct was the major on-call pharmacist after hours for local hospice, nursing homes and assisted living centers. Ms. Fisher does own fifty percent of Fisher or she did until her former partners did an illegal conversion of Fisher Rx Direct with the help of Alliance Bank & Trust thru an inequitable assertion of power or position. Examples of inequitable assertions of power in this case are: taking Ms. Fisher's name off the Fisher Rx Direct bank account, selling the major asset, which is the Fisher Rx Direct patient files and pocketing the money, refusing to allow Ms. Fisher to practice pharmacy in her own pharmacy, refusing to allow Ms. Fisher access to the financial records of Fisher Rx Direct after the illegal conversion, and refusing to allow Ms. Fisher access to the Fisher Rx Direct bank account unless she signed the buyout agreement and Alliance Bank & Trust sided with former partners and continued to refuse to give her access to all bank statements which can be used as evidence in the complaint. Alliance Bank & Trust is jointly and severally liable because they allowed John Whaley and Carl Whaley to an inequitable assertion of power over Fisher Rx Direct by allowing Carl and John Whaley to treat Fisher Rx Direct as if they were 100% owners of Fisher Rx Direct, instead of only 50% partners. The Fisher Rx Direct account should have been frozen until this lawsuit is finished. Alliance Bank & Trust did not treat Ms. Fisher as a fifty percent partner in Fisher Rx Direct. John Whaley being on the Board of Directors of Alliance Bank & Trust is both an aggravating factor and an egregious factor in this case because of what Alliance Bank & Trust allowed Carl and John Whaley to do. After Ms. Fisher's former partners refused to allow her back into her own pharmacy to practice pharmacy, they no longer allowed an on-call pharmacist after hours for hospices, nursing homes, and assisted living centers that were being served and are examples of the tort of interference with an existing contract. Ms. Fisher has made several contacts with potential patients and patient groups and they were willing to transfer business to Fisher Rx Direct pharmacy once she was back working as a pharmacist at her own pharmacy which is an example of the tort of interference of prospective potential contracts. Ms. Fisher will be able to provide statements from the prospective clients as proof during discovery and at trial. The following are proof of actual injuries in this case: Ms. Fisher lost the use of Fisher Rx Direct which is a specific and unique property; Ms. Fisher lost wages and she also lost the use of her own personal bank account among other things which will be presented in the discovery process.

Ms. Fisher prays for the court to not dismiss any original claim against John Whaley, Carl Whaley, Choice Med, INC, and Alliance Bank & Trust in the interest of justice.

STATE OF NORTH CAROLINA
COUNTY OF CLEVELAND
FILE NO: 13 CVS 579

Cynthia Ann Fisher
        Plaintiff

vs.

Choice Med INC, Carl Whaley,

John Whaley, and Alliance Bank &
Trust (Defendants)

Motion to Dismiss Counterclaim of John Whaley and Opposition to
Motion to Dismiss Complaint of Plaintiff Cynthia Ann Fisher
Now comes the Plaintiff Cynthia Ann Fisher by and through the
undersigned counsel, pursuant to Rules 8 and 12 of the North
Carolina Rules of Civil Procedure. Ms. Fisher is alleging several
violations of North Carolina General Statute 75-1.1 in opposition to
Motion to Dismiss. Ms. Fisher is enclosing a copy of her valid
pharmacy license, copy of purchase/sell agreement, and buyout
contact. Ms. Fisher will provide more proof through the discovery
process of unpaid bills and unauthorized transfer of funds by the
defendant Carl Whaley. Ms. Fisher is also attaching a Memorandum
of Law in Opposition to Motion to Dismiss. Ms. Fisher can provide
witnesses whom will attest to the integrity and honesty of Ms.
Fisher's character. The District Attorney dismissed the alleged
charges of forgery and fraud John and Carl Whaley brought against
Ms. Fisher due to the unsubstantiated claims of Carl and John
Whaley. Qualified privilege is not allowed because the allegations
were dismissed by the District Attorney. Examples of character
witnesses that Ms. Fisher can provide are stellar members of the
Cleveland County Community and includes: Dr. Jim Potts, MD,
Director of Hospice of Cleveland County, Ms. Fern Potts, she is a

pharmacist at Cleveland Regional Medical Center, Dr. Forest Thompson, MD, Oncologist, Hematology Specialist and his wife Lisa Thompson, and Fr. Michael Kottar, priest of St. Mary's Catholic Church, located in Shelby, NC. Ms. Fisher can provide several more names of character witnesses through the discovery process. Ms. Fisher is fifty percent owner of all contracts and property of Fisher Rx Direct, LLC and she has the right to protect these interests. The defendant's conduct is not privileged because his conduct is not lawful and not consistent with community standard. The conduct of Carl Whaley in this matter was in bad faith not good faith. Also, in violations of NC General Statute 75-1.1, the alleged good faith of the defendant does not matter. Ms. Fisher tried to save her company and attempted to buy it back but she could not sign the unconscionable buyout contract. The enclosed copy of the buyout agreement will show how unfair it was. Ms. Fisher did not rely on it but it is proof of the value that the defendant put on the pharmacy. Ms. Fisher has a perfectly valid pharmacy license and she is enclosing a copy of the pharmacy license and the court may verify the license at the NC BOP website. Ms. Fisher is also currently working at as a retail pharmacist. If Ms. Fisher had lost her license she would not be able to work as a pharmacist. Employee theft was discovered in June 2011, much to the dismay of Ms. Fisher and employee-pharmacist, Mr. Stan Pitts, RPh. In July 2011, Ms. Fisher asked Stan Pitts to become the official pharmacy manager in her place and he agreed and Ms. Fisher continued working as a staff pharmacist and owner. Stan Pitts was the Fisher Rx Direct pharmacy manager until the Defendants Carl and John Whaley closed the pharmacy in July 2012. Ms. Fisher is enclosing a copy of the Buyout agreement that Defendants Carl and John Whaley tried to get Ms. Fisher to sign after selling the patient files. Ms. Fisher does not have a copy of the check written for the Fisher Rx Direct patient files because both the Defendants Carl Whaley and John Whaley and their attorney Joshua Farmer have consistently refused to give a copy to Ms. Fisher. Ms. Fisher is alleging criminal embezzlement until she sees a copy of the check written for the purchase of Fisher Rx Direct patient files. If the check is written to anyone besides Fisher Rx Direct and deposited in any account except Fisher Rx Direct, that is criminal embezzlement. Ms. Fisher will give the court any copies of current paid check stubs to provide proof of what she is currently making as a pharmacist. Defendants Carl and John Whaley have refused to give Ms. Fisher her private property. Some of the private property included family pictures, which did not belong to Fisher Rx Direct but to Ms. Fisher privately.

Answer and Motion to Dismiss Counterclaim of John Whaley

Pursuant to Rule 12(b)(6) of the North Carolina Rules of Civil Procedure, Plaintiff Cynthia Ann Fisher moves to dismiss the counterclaims raised against her by Defendant in this matter. The counterclaim filed by Defendant fails to state a claim against Plaintiff upon which relief may be granted. Ms. Fisher is enclosing a copy of the Buy/Sell agreement to prove that Carl Whaley and John Whaley bought fifty percent of Fisher Rx Direct under Whaley Communications. The name Whaley Communications is now Choice Med Inc. There are several contradictory statements made by the defendant. The defendant seems to think that Ms. Fisher would let someone have fifty percent of her company for borrowing money. Ms. Fisher did not borrow any money but she did sell fifty percent of her company. The defendant appears to be using language interchangeably that should not be used interchangeably.

1. Pursuant to rule 8(b) of the Federal Rules of Civil Procedure, Ms. Fisher is denying each and every allegation contained in Defendant's counterclaim, if the court finds that the defendant has stated a claim for which relief may be granted.
2. Ms. Fisher reserves the right to assert at trail such other and further defenses as may be learned thru the discovery process or otherwise.

3. Ms. Fisher is alleging the counterclaim is malicious and frivolous under NC General Statute section 75-1.1.
4. If the court finds that some of these allegations need to be brought by Fisher Rx Direct, Ms. Fisher will do another complaint on behalf of her fifty percent interest in Fisher Rx Direct against all parties involved or add Fisher Rx Direct as a third party plaintiff against all defendants with the permission of the court.
5. Ms. Fisher would also like to requests the court's permission to add Masters Pharmaceuticals as a third party plaintiff against all the defendants. Master's Pharmaceuticals has a complaint against Fisher Rx Direct and Ms. Fisher herself because her former partners refused to pay Masters for medicine ordered when Ms. Fisher was not in control of Fisher Rx Direct, due to the illegal conversion of Fisher Rx Direct by former partners.
6. Ms. Fisher requests a motion to strike under rule 12(f), pursuant to the Federal Rules of Civil Procedure, the accusation that her pharmacy license is permanently suspended because it is impertinent, scandalous, and prejudicial because it is untrue. Ms. Fisher is currently working as a licensed pharmacist with full NC Board approval. According to *Garlock v. Henson, 112 N.C. App. 243, 435 S.E.2d 114 (1993)*, lying is considered an aggravating circumstance under the NC General Statute 75-1.1.

Ms. Fisher prays for the following relief from the court:
7. Ms. Fisher requests an accounting of all diverted funds the Defendants John and Carl Whaley diverted.
8. Ms. Fisher requests a copy of check written for the purchase of Fisher Rx Direct patient files and proof of where the money is.

9. Ms. Fisher requests copies of all bank statements from Alliance Bank & Trust and all cancelled checks written for bills and anything else.
10. Ms. Fisher is willing to go to court and she desires to attach several violations of NC General Statutes 75-1.1, instead of using the common law tort theory when assessing damages at trial.
11. Ms. Fisher respectfully asks the court for costs and reasonable attorney fees to be taxed against defendant.
12. Ms. Fisher respectfully asks the court for such other and further relief as the court deems just and proper.
13. Ms. Fisher respectfully asks the court that the costs of this matter be taxed to the defendant.
14. Ms. Fisher respectfully asks the court that her lost wages be taxed to the defendant.
15. Ms. Fisher respectfully asks the court that any bank fees, returned check fees, and late fees caused by the actions of the defendant be taxed against the defendant.
16. Ms. Fisher respectfully asks for a trial by jury on all issues so triable.
17. Ms. Fisher respectfully asks the court to dismiss all counterclaims of defendant John Whaley with prejudice.
18. Ms. Fisher respectfully asks the court, if possible to use compensation and damages awarded to Ms. Fisher after unpaid debts are cleared up concerning Fisher Rx Direct and Ms. Fisher caused by the actions of Defendants against Ms. Fisher, to help in the establishment of a Legal Aid clinic in Cleveland County to help anyone that is hurt by the actions of another and does not know what to do and needs help.

STATE OF NORTH CAROLINA
COUNTY OF CLEVELAND

Cynthia Ann Fisher
                    Plaintiff

vs.

Choice Med INC, Carl Whaley,

John Whaley, and Alliance Bank &
Trust   (Defendants)

Opposition to Motion to Dismiss Complaint of Plaintiff Cynthia Ann
Fisher (13 CVS 579)

Now comes the Plaintiff Cynthia Ann Fisher by and through the
undersigned counsel, pursuant to Rules 8 and 12 of the North
Carolina Rules of Civil Procedure. Ms. Fisher is alleging several
violations of North Carolina General Statute 75-1.1 in opposition to
Motion to Dismiss. Ms. Fisher is enclosing a copy of her valid
pharmacy license, copy of purchase/sell agreement, and buyout
contact. Ms. Fisher will provide more proof through the discovery
process of unpaid bills and unauthorized transfer of funds by the
defendant Carl Whaley. Ms. Fisher is also attaching a Memorandum
of Law in Opposition to Motion to Dismiss. Ms. Fisher can provide
witnesses whom will attest to the integrity and honesty of Ms.
Fisher's character. The District Attorney dismissed the alleged
charges of forgery and fraud John and Carl Whaley brought against
Ms. Fisher due to the unsubstantiated claims of Carl and John
Whaley. Qualified privilege is not allowed because the allegations
were dismissed by the District Attorney. Examples of character
witnesses that Ms. Fisher can provide are stellar members of the
Cleveland County Community and includes: Dr. Jim Potts, MD,

Director of Hospice of Cleveland County, Ms. Fern Potts, she is a pharmacist at Cleveland Regional Medical Center, Dr. Forest Thompson, MD, Oncologist, Hematology Specialist and his wife Lisa Thompson, and Fr. Michael Kottar, priest of St. Mary's Catholic Church, located in Shelby, NC. Ms. Fisher can provide several more names of character witnesses through the discovery process. Ms. Fisher is fifty percent owner of all contracts and property of Fisher Rx Direct, LLC and she has the right to protect these interests. The defendant's conduct is not privileged because his conduct is not lawful and not consistent with community standard. The conduct of Carl Whaley in this matter was in bad faith not good faith. Also, in violations of NC General Statute 75-1.1, the alleged good faith of the defendant does not matter. Ms. Fisher tried to save her company and attempted to buy it back but she could not sign the unconscionable buyout contract. The enclosed copy of the buyout agreement will show how unfair it was. Ms. Fisher did not rely on it but it is proof of the value that the defendant put on the pharmacy. Ms. Fisher has a perfectly valid pharmacy license and she is enclosing a copy of the pharmacy license and the court may verify the license at the NC BOP website. Ms. Fisher is also currently working at as a retail pharmacist. If Ms. Fisher had lost her license she would not be able to work as a pharmacist. Employee theft was discovered in June 2011, much to the dismay of Ms. Fisher and employee-pharmacist, Mr. Stan Pitts, RPh. In July 2011, Ms. Fisher asked Stan Pitts to become the official pharmacy manager in her place and he agreed and Ms. Fisher continued working as a staff pharmacist and owner. Stan Pitts was the Fisher Rx Direct pharmacy manager until the Defendants Carl and John Whaley closed the pharmacy in July 2012. Ms. Fisher is enclosing a copy of the Buyout agreement that Defendants Carl and John Whaley tried to get Ms. Fisher to sign after selling the patient files. Ms. Fisher does not have a copy of the check written for the Fisher Rx Direct patient files because both the Defendants Carl Whaley and John Whaley and their attorney Joshua Farmer have consistently refused to give a copy to Ms. Fisher. Ms. Fisher is alleging criminal embezzlement until she sees a copy of the check written for the purchase of Fisher Rx Direct patient files. If the check is written to anyone besides Fisher Rx Direct and deposited in any account except Fisher Rx Direct, that is criminal embezzlement. Ms. Fisher will give the court any copies of current paid check stubs to provide proof of what she is currently making as a pharmacist. Defendants Carl and John Whaley have refused to give Ms. Fisher her private property. Some of the private property included family pictures, which did not belong to Fisher Rx Direct but to Ms. Fisher privately.

Answer and Motion to Dismiss Counterclaim of Carl Whaley

Pursuant to Rule 12(b)(6) of the North Carolina Rules of Civil Procedure, Plaintiff Cynthia Ann Fisher moves to dismiss the counterclaims raised against her by Defendant in this matter. The counterclaim filed by Defendant fails to state a claim against Plaintiff upon which relief may be granted. Ms. Fisher is enclosing a copy of the Buy/Sell agreement to prove that Carl Whaley and John Whaley bought fifty percent of Fisher Rx Direct under Whaley Communications. The name Whaley Communications is now Choice Med Inc. There are several contradictory statements made by the defendant. The defendant seems to think that Ms. Fisher would let someone have fifty percent of her company for borrowing money. Ms. Fisher did not borrow any money but she did sell fifty percent of her company. The defendant appears to be using language interchangeably that should not be used interchangeably.

1. Pursuant to rule 8(b) of the Federal Rules of Civil Procedure, Ms. Fisher is denying each and every allegation contained in Defendant's counterclaim, if the court finds that the defendant has stated a claim for which relief may be granted.
2. Ms. Fisher reserves the right to assert at trail such other and further defenses as may be learned thru the discovery process or otherwise.

3. Ms. Fisher is alleging the counterclaim is malicious and frivolous under NC General Statute section 75-1.1.

4. If the court finds that some of these allegations need to be brought by Fisher Rx Direct, Ms. Fisher will do another complaint on behalf of her fifty percent interest in Fisher Rx Direct against all parties involved or add Fisher Rx Direct as a third party plaintiff against all defendants with the permission of the court.

5. Ms. Fisher would also like to requests the court's permission to add Masters Pharmaceuticals as a third party plaintiff against all the defendants. Master's Pharmaceuticals has a complaint against Fisher Rx Direct and Ms. Fisher herself because her former partners refused to pay Masters for medicine ordered when Ms. Fisher was not in control of Fisher Rx Direct, due to the illegal conversion of Fisher Rx Direct by former partners.

6. Ms. Fisher requests a motion to strike under rule 12(f), pursuant to the Federal Rules of Civil Procedure, the accusation that her pharmacy license is permanently suspended because it is impertinent, scandalous, and prejudicial because it is untrue. Ms. Fisher is currently working as a licensed pharmacist with full NC Board approval. According to *Garlock v. Henson, 112 N.C. App. 243, 435 S.E.2d 114 (1993),* lying is considered an aggravating circumstance under the NC General Statute 75-1.1.

Ms. Fisher prays for the following relief from the court:

7. Ms. Fisher requests an accounting of all diverted funds the Defendants John and Carl Whaley diverted.

8. Ms. Fisher requests a copy of check written for the purchase of Fisher Rx Direct patient files and proof of where the money is.

9. Ms. Fisher requests copies of all bank statements from Alliance Bank & Trust and all cancelled checks written for bills and anything else.
10. Ms. Fisher is willing to go to court and she desires to attach several violations of NC General Statutes 75-1.1, instead of using the common law tort theory when assessing damages at trial.
11. Ms. Fisher respectfully asks the court for costs and reasonable attorney fees to be taxed against defendant.
12. Ms. Fisher respectfully asks the court for such other and further relief as the court deems just and proper.
13. Ms. Fisher respectfully asks the court that the costs of this matter be taxed to the defendant.
14. Ms. Fisher respectfully asks the court that her lost wages be taxed to the defendant.
15. Ms. Fisher respectfully asks the court that any bank fees, returned check fees, and late fees caused by the actions of the defendant be taxed against the defendant.
16. Ms. Fisher respectfully asks for a trial by jury on all issues so triable.
17. Ms. Fisher respectfully asks the court to dismiss all counterclaims of defendant Carl Whaley with prejudice.
18. Ms. Fisher respectfully asks the court, if possible to use compensation and damages awarded to Ms. Fisher after unpaid debts are cleared up concerning Fisher Rx Direct and Ms. Fisher caused by the actions of Defendants against Ms. Fisher, to help in the establishment of a Legal Aid clinic in Cleveland County to help anyone that is hurt by the actions of another and does not know what to do and needs help.

Appendix C Court paper concerning Cynthia Fisher v. Community Pharmacy (15-CVS-1141) (Superior Court Division: Cleveland County), Shelby NC

Dr. Cynthia A. Fisher

    Vs.

Community Pharmacy
(Owners, Registered Agents, Managers)

Complaint

Comes now the Plaintiff Dr. Cynthia A. Fisher and files this her complaint against Community Pharmacy (owners, registered agents, managers). Dr. Fisher is a resident of Cleveland County and lives in Shelby, NC. Community Pharmacy is an independent drug store located in Shelby NC.   Community Pharmacy conducts business as a drug store in Cleveland County.

Fisher Rx Direct was an independent pharmacy owned and operated by Dr. Cynthia A. Fisher from 2007-2012. John, Carl, and Harriet Whaley became partners with Dr. Fisher in 2009. Dr. Fisher and the Whaley's were fifty-fifty concerning the ownership of Fisher Rx Direct

In the law of intentional torts ignorance of the law is no excuse.

Issue: Tort of Conversion

Rule: The tort of conversion occurs when the Defendant substantially interferes with the Plaintiff's possession or ownership of property that it is fair to require the Defendant to pay the property's fair value.

Analysis: Community Pharmacy (owners, registered agents, managers) substantially interfered with Dr. Fisher's ownership of Fisher Rx Direct when they retained ownership of the patient files and other assets of Fisher Rx Direct without the written or verbal permission of Dr. Fisher.

Conclusion: Community Pharmacy owes Dr. Fisher the full value of Fisher Rx Direct because Community Pharmacy committed the tort of Conversion when they conspired with the Whaley's to steal the patient files and assets of Fisher Rx Direct. Dr. Fisher never gave the Whaley's written or verbal permission to sale the patient files and assets of Fisher Rx Direct.

Issue: Inducing breach of contract

Rule: An intentional act that causes a third person to breach an existing contract with the Plaintiff.

Analysis: Community Pharmacy (owners/registered agents/managers) committed an intentional act when they purchased the patient files and other assets of Fisher Rx Direct from John and Ms. Fisher was fifty percent owner of Fisher Rx Direct and the Whaley's owned fifty percent of Fisher Rx Direct. The Whaley's include Harriet, John, and Carl Whaley. Community Pharmacy induced the Whaley's to breach their contract with Dr. Fisher. Community knew that Dr. Fisher was one of the owners of Fisher Rx Direct.

Conclusion: Community Pharmacy owes Dr. Fisher compensation and punitive damages for inducing the Whaley's to breach their contract with Dr. Fisher when they agreed to purchase Fisher Rx Direct patient files and other assets from the Whaley's without her written permission. Dr. Fisher did not authorize the sale of patient files and other assets of Fisher Rx Direct.

Issue: Interference with contractual relations

Rule: Even if the interference does not cause contractual breach, Defendant may be liable if his interference makes performance under the contract substantially more difficult.

Analysis: Community Pharmacy (owners/registered agents/managers) interfered with Dr. Fisher's contractual relation with the Whaley's when they purchased Fisher Rx Direct patient files and other assets without Dr. Fisher's written or verbal permission. Community pharmacy knew that Dr. Fisher was one of the owners

Conclusion: Community Pharmacy owes Dr. Fisher compensation and punitive damages for interference with Dr. Fisher's contractual relations with the Whaley's when they agreed to purchase Fisher Rx Direct patient files and other assets from the Whaley's without her written permission. Dr. Fisher did not authorize the sale of patient files and other assets of Fisher Rx Direct.

Issue: Interference with Prospective economic advantage:

Rule: A defendant may be liable for interfering with Plaintiff's expectation of economic benefit from third persons even in the absence of an existing contract.

Analysis: Community Pharmacy (owners/registered agents/managers) conspired with John and Carl Whaley to deprive Dr. Cynthia A. Fisher from her ownership of Fisher Rx Direct. Community Pharmacy bought the patient files and other assets of Fisher Rx Direct without written or verbal authorization from Dr. Cynthia A. Fisher. The Whaley's did not have Dr. Fisher's permission to sale the patient files and other assets of Fisher Rx Direct. Dr. Fisher received no compensation from Community Pharmacy when they obtained the files illegally. Community Pharmacy knew that Dr. Fisher was part owner of Fisher Rx Direct.

Conclusion: Community Pharmacy owes Dr. Fisher compensation and punitive damages for the patient assets and files that Community Pharmacy stole from Fisher Rx Direct. By stealing the patient files and other assets from Fisher Rx Direct, Community Pharmacy interfered with Dr. Fisher's prospective economic advantage from Fisher Rx Direct.

Issue: Intentional Infliction of Emotional Distress

Rule: Intentional and extreme outrageous conduct that causes injury (physical harm not required). Defendant desires to cause Plaintiff emotional distress; Defendant knows with substantial certainty that Plaintiff will suffer emotional distress; or Defendant recklessly disregards the high probability that emotional distress will occur. According to the Third Restatement a person recklessly causes harm created by his or her conduct or know facts that make that risk obvious to anyone in the plaintiff's situation and the precaution that would eliminate or reduce that risk involves burdens that are so slight relative to the magnitude of the risk as to render highly blameworthy the Defendant's failure to adopt the precaution.

Analysis: In the case of Dr. Fisher, Community Pharmacy (owners, registered agents, managers) knew that Dr. Fisher did not know that the Whaley's were selling the patient files and other assets of Fisher Rx Direct without her knowledge or should have verified that information before purchasing the patient files and other assets. Dr. Fisher lives in Shelby, NC and Community Pharmacy is located in Shelby, NC. All Community Pharmacy had to do was call Dr. Fisher to verify anything and Community Pharmacy did not do that.

Conclusion: Community Pharmacy owes Dr. Fisher compensation and punitive damages for the loss of Fisher Rx Direct due to reckless behavior in purchasing the patient files and other assets of Fisher Rx Direct without her written or verbal permission and knowledge. Dr. Fisher suffered severe emotional and mental distress due to the loss of her business.

Issue: Negligent infliction of Emotional Distress

Rule: You owe a duty of care to all people who are foreseeable victims of your failure to take precautions.

Analysis: Community Pharmacy (owners, registered agents, managers) knew that Dr. Fisher was a foreseeable victim in their complicit behavior with the Whaley's. : In the case of Dr. Fisher, Community Pharmacy (owner, registered agents, managers) knew that Dr. Fisher did not know that the Whaley's were selling the patient files and other assets of Fisher Rx Direct without her knowledge and should have verified that information before purchasing the patient files and other assets. Dr. Fisher lives in Shelby, NC and Community Pharmacy is located in Shelby, NC. All Community Pharmacy had to do was call Dr. Fisher to verify anything and Community Pharmacy did not do that.

Conclusion: Community Pharmacy owes Dr. Fisher compensation and punitive damages for the loss of Fisher Rx Direct due to reckless behavior in purchasing the patient files and other assets of Fisher Rx Direct without her written or verbal permission and knowledge. Dr. Fisher suffered severe emotional and mental distress due to the loss of her business.

Plaintiff Dr. Cynthia A. Fisher prays to the court:

WHEREFORE PREMISES CONSIDERED, Plaintiff demands a judgement of $1,000,000 dollars in actual damages and $3,000,000 in punitive damages.

Dr. Fisher had no choice but to declare personal bankruptcy because of the loss of her pharmacy. Dr. Fisher received no compensation when Community Pharmacy was able to get control of Fisher Rx Direct patient files and other Fisher Rx Direct assets. By not verifying that Dr. Fisher was willing to sale the patient files and the other assets of her business Community Pharmacy is and was guilty of deceitful business practices.

Plaintiff Dr. Cynthia A. Fisher prays for such other relief as in law or equity she may be entitled.

This the 20th day of July 2015.

Respectfully submitted,

_____

Dr. Cynthia A. Fisher
Vs.
Community Pharmacy
(Also known as Shelby Family Pharmacy)

To: Wesley L. Deaton
Attorney for the Defendant
PO Box 2459
Denver, NC 28037

FIRST SET OF ADMISSIONS

1. Admit that the sale of the patient file and assets of Fisher Rx Direct, LLC occurred on July 17, 2012.

   I can neither admit nor deny this because Fisher Rx Direct was closed on July 22, 2012. That is when the statute of limitations started to run from what I understand because that is when all transactions took place or maybe took place the next day. I was not informed of anything because I was kept out of Fisher Rx Direct illegally by the Whaleys.

2. Admit that Fisher Rx Direct, LLC was the owner of the patient files and assets that were sold to Community Pharmacy.

I do admit that Fisher Rx Direct, LLC was the owner of the patient files and assets of Community Pharmacy. However, I owned fifty percent (50%) of Fisher Rx Direct, LLC.

3. Admit Whaley Communications, LLC held a 50 percent (50%) membership interest in Fisher Rx Direct, LLC.

    Whaley Communications did own 50 percent (50%) of Fisher Rx Direct but they did not own 100 percent (100%), I also owned 50 percent (50%) of Fisher Rx Direct, LLC.

4. Admit that Carl Whaley was a manager of Fisher Rx Direct, LLC.

    I do admit that Carl Whaley and I were co-managers of Fisher Rx Direct, LLC. We shared the responsibility. I told him that he could make no decisions unless he consulted me. He tried to coerce me to sign an unfair buy-out agreement. When I would not sign the agreement he then sold the pharmacy files and other assets to Community Pharmacy from what I understand.

5. Admit that the Defendant only agreed to purchase patient file and assets of Fisher Rx Direct after Don Beam a member of the Defendant, was contact by the Whaleys offering to sell the Defendant said files and assets on behalf of Fisher Rx Direct, LLC.

    I can neither admit nor deny this because I was not consulted on selling the patient files or assets to Community Pharmacy. Carl Whaley did not have my permission to sell the patient files and other assets of Fisher Rx Direct, LLC, to Community Pharmacy.

6. Admit that Fisher Rx Direct, LLC, was to be involuntarily closed when the Whaleys contacted Mr. Beam.

I can neither admit nor deny this because the Whaleys did not contact me and tell me that the pharmacy had to be involuntarily closed. If was to be involuntarily closed why did the Whaleys try to coerce me into signing an unfair buy-out agreement.

7. Admit that the pending closure of Fisher Rx Direct, LLC, was why the Whaleys approached Don Beam, a member of the Defendant about the opportunity to purchase patient files and assets of the pharmacy from Fisher Rx Direct, LLC.

I can neither admit nor deny this because the Whaleys tried to coerce me into signing an unfair buyout agreement. If they were trying to get me to buyout the pharmacy it should not have had to be involuntarily closed. Or if it was to be involuntarily closed I should have been told about this and they should not have tried to get me to buyout a pharmacy that had to be involuntarily closed. I did have an attorney at this time and she told me not to sign the agreement also

NORTH CAROLINA
CLEVELAND COUNTY
CYNTHIA A. FISHER
PLAINTIFF,
Vs,
COMMUNITY PHARMACY,
DEFENDANT

DEFENDANT'S FIRST SET OF REQUEST FOR ADMISSIONS

TO: Wesley L. Deaton
Attorney for Defendant

P.O. Box 2459
Denver, NC 28037

NOW COMES THE PLAINTIFF, by and thru pro se, and pursuant to rule 36 of the North Carolina Rules of Civil Procedure and serves the following Requests for Admission upon the Defendant:

These Requests for Admissions are served upon you pursuant to Rule 36 of the Rules of Civil Procedure. You are reminded that pursuant to Rule 37 (c) of the Rules of Civil Procedure entitled "Expenses on Failure to Admit, "if you fail to admit to the genuineness of any document or the truth of the matter as requested under Rule 36, and if the Plaintiff thereafter proves the genuineness of the document or the truth of the matter, Plaintiff may apply to the Court for an order requiring you to pay reasonable expenses incurred in making that proof, including attorney's fees.

You are requested to admit for the purpose of this action only, within thirty (30) days of service hereof:

ADMISSIONS

1. Admit that Fisher Rx Direct, LLC, did not close its doors until July 22, 2012 and that is when the Statute of Limitations began.

   Admit____   Deny_____

2. Admit that Cynthia Fisher was fifty percent owner of Fisher Rx Direct, LLC when the patient files and assets were sold to Community Pharmacy.

   Admit____   Deny_____

3. Admit that Cynthia Fisher did not sign anything for her fifty percent ownership to be sold to Community Pharmacy.

Admit_____   Deny_____

4. Admit that Whaley Communications, LLC, owned fifty percent of Fisher Rx Direct, LLC, but not 100 hundred percent.

   Admit_____   Deny_____

5. Admit that Carl Whaley did not have Cynthia Fisher's permission to sell her part of Fisher Rx Direct, LLC.

   Admit_____   Deny_____

6. Admit that Carl Whaley was a co-manager with Cynthia Fisher and could not take any action without her approval.

   Admit_____   Deny_____

7. Admit that Carl Whaley did not have Cynthia Fisher's approval to sell the patient files and assets to Community Pharmacy.

   Admit_____   Deny_____

8. Admit that Cynthia Fisher was not aware that Fisher Rx Direct was to be involuntarily closed because Carl and John Whaley kept Cynthia Fisher out of her pharmacy illegally.

   Admit_____   Deny_____

9. Admit that Carl and John Whaley attempted to coerce Cynthia Fisher to sign an unfair buyout agreement and sold the patient files and assets out from under her and pocketed the money when she refused to be coerced.

Admit_____ Deny_____

10. Admit that no one from Community Pharmacy attempted to contact Cynthia Fisher to verify that Carl and John Whaley had the legal right to sell 100 percent of the patient files and assets of Fisher Rx Direct, LLC, without the signature of Cynthia Fisher.

Admit_____ Deny_____

11. Admit that neither Carl nor John Whaley had the legal right to sell 100 percent of patient files and assets of Fisher Rx Direct, LLC because Cynthia Fisher did not give them the right and they only had a fifty percent ownership of Fisher Rx Direct, LLC.

Admit_____ Deny_____

12. Admit that Cynthia Fisher attempted to get a copy of the check written to Carl and John Whaley for the patient files and other assets of Fisher Rx Direct, LLC. Billy Wease was approached for this information and his response was that he did not want to get involved. This was attempted in 2012 or 2013.

Admit_____ Deny_____

Dr. Cynthia A. Fisher
Vs.

Community Pharmacy
(Also known as Shelby Family Pharmacy)

Motion to Compel Documents Requested and motion to deny attorney fees requested

Dr. Fisher was within the statute of limitations because Fisher Rx Direct did not close its doors until July 22, 2012. The patient files and other assets of Fisher Rx Direct was transferred to Community Pharmacy (also known as Shelby Family Pharmacy) at the Secretary of State website. Dr. Fisher filed the subpoena on July 20, 2015. Within the statute of limitations guidelines as far as she knows. The name on the front of the building is Community Pharmacy and that is the only name that Dr. Fisher knew the pharmacy by until their attorney sent her a copy of the motion to quash the subpoena. The registered agent is Debra K. Griffin. The official name on the NC Secretary of State website is Shelby Family Pharmacy.

Dr. Fisher has no problem giving Community Pharmacy or Shelby Family Pharmacy which ever name the pharmacy officially goes by until September 1, for the production of the requested documents in the subpoena.

The assets from the sale of Fisher Rx Direct patient files and other assets to Community Pharmacy (Shelby Family Pharmacy) were included in Dr. Fisher's chapter 7 bankruptcy. The trustee of the Chapter 7 bankruptcy settled the civil case against Carl and John Whaley, and Med Choice Inc. Dr. Fisher had a civil case pending that became part of her bankrupt estate. Dr. Fisher can prove everything concerning her bankruptcy. Her bankruptcy attorney was Mr. Gardner here in Shelby, NC. Dr. Fisher had to file a Chapter 7 bankruptcy because Carl Whaley and John Whaley stole her business and then sold the patient files and assets of Fisher Rx Direct to Community Pharmacy (or Shelby Family Pharmacy). Dr.

Fisher did not find out that the patient files and other assets were sold until after her business was closed.

Carl and John Whaley allegedly committed a class C felony against Dr. Fisher. Dr. Fisher has not went to the District Attorney yet concerning the embezzlement. Dr. Fisher had to get copies of bank records herself and it only cost her $133.00. So it is not oppressive because of the expense.

The subpoena was signed by the clerk of superior court at the Cleveland County courthouse and was served by the Sheriff. So the subpoena was served properly.

Dr. Fisher is not a licensed attorney yet but she does have an Executive Juris Doctor degree. So she does have a law degree. Dr. Fisher is apologizing to the court for mistakes she makes because she is still learning.

Dr. Fisher is praying to the court for a motion to compel documents requested and to deny the attorney fees.

Certificate of Service
File No: 15 CVS 1141

This certifies that a copy of the foregoing has been served upon the following by being placed in the United States Mail, postage prepaid, addressed as follows:

From what Dr. Fisher can gather Community Pharmacy is Shelby Family Pharmacy according to the Secretary of State website. This is confusing because the name on the building is Community Pharmacy.

Wesley L. Deaton
Attorney for Shelby Family Pharmacy, Inc.,
PO Box 2459
Denver, NC 28037
704-489-2491
State Bar No. 25395

This the 8th day of October, 2015.

Dr. Cynthia A. Fisher, PharmD, EJD

Cynthia Ann Fisher
(Plaintiff)

Vs.

Community Pharmacy
(Defendant)

Opposition to Motion to Dismiss and Memorandum of Law

Now Comes the Plaintiff thru Pro Se, is opposing the motion to dismiss because it is now being handled by the Bankruptcy of the Plaintiff. Dr. Fisher has had her bankruptcy attorney to reopen her bankruptcy to add this complaint as an asset.

Dr. Fisher is also asking for the attorney fees she had to spend for the bankruptcy and the reopening the bankruptcy. Community Pharmacy was instrumental in causing her to declare bankruptcy. Dr. Fisher has filed a criminal complaint for everything that took place in 13-CVS-579 and 15-CVS-1141. She filed the initial complaint thru the police department and it has now been given to the District Attorney for investigation. J. D. Ruppe was the officer who took the complaint and gave it the District Attorney.

Dr. Fisher is not even sure if she can do the opposition to Motion to Dismiss anymore because it is part of her bankruptcy.
The amount that Dr. Fisher has spent on her bankruptcy so far including reopening the bankruptcy is $3045.00. Dr. Fisher would like reimbursement of her bankruptcy attorney fees if possible because Community Pharmacy was instrumental in her bankruptcy

Dr. Fisher is praying to the court for relief of the attorney fees she has had to spend on bankruptcy so far. If Dr. Fisher is wrong about the amount but she correct it but she does have copies of all canceled checks and she can get copies of everything from her bankruptcy attorney.

She does know that all defendants in the two complaints 13-CVS-579 and 15-CVS-1141 together forced her into bankruptcy. She believes that would come under the Unfair Trade Practice Act. Dr. Fisher has requested a copy of the check or checks written to Carl and John Whaley for the patient files and other assets that was bought by Community Pharmacy both formally and informally. Dr. Fisher still has not received the copy of the check yet. From what Dr. Fisher understands there are some things that you should be able to receive without a formal request for production of documents. Dr. Fisher might not have made the request for the production of documents, but she did request them. Hopefully, the District Attorney, can get a copy of the checks written to Carl and John Whaley by Community Pharmacy for patient files and other assets of Fisher Rx Direct, thru his investigation.
I pray that I am doing everything properly until the Bankruptcy court decides how to handle this.

Appendix D Court papers concerning Cynthia Fisher v Thomas Norkus, William Joe Goodman,

David and Emily Williams (15-CVS-610; Superior Court Division: Cleveland County, Shelby NC)

Complaint: Fraud; Conspiracy to Commit Fraud; Negligent and Intentional Infliction of Emotional Distress
Cynthia Fisher v. Thomas Norkus, Emily Williams, David Williams, and William Joe Goodman
Pursuant to the Federal and North Carolina rules of civil procedure, the complaint and background are described to the following paragraphs.

Thomas Norkus
Issue: Did Thomas Norkus commit intentional misrepresentation (fraud) to Dr. Fisher?
Rule: An intent to induce the plaintiff's reliance on the misrepresentation.
Analysis: Dr. Fisher relied on the fact that Thomas Norkus was not cheating on her because he never told her he wanted to start dating other people. She also let him know that if he started dating other people she would move and cut him out of her life. Thomas Norkus became involved in an adulterous affair with Emily Williams. Emily Williams is the wife of David Williams. Dr. Fisher became aware of the affair in September 2014 when she caught Mrs. Williams with Thomas Norkus on the security camera in Dr. Fisher and Thomas Norkus home. Thomas Norkus new about and agreed to the security cameras. When Dr. Fisher confronted him, he told her that she would not have seen anything if the security cameras had not been installed.
Conclusion: Thomas Norkus owes Dr. Fisher compensatory damages in excess of $15,000 because of the money Dr. Fisher spent on him and his house in 2014. Dr. Fisher would not have spent any money on Thomas Norkus if she had known about the adulterous affair because she would not have been around. Dr. Fisher would have moved out. Thomas Norkus is the proximate cause of Dr. Fisher's financial harm.

Issue: Did Thomas Norkus cause Dr. Fisher negligent and intentional mental and emotional distress because of his involvement in an adulterous affair behind her back and using her and lying to her.

Rule: The tort of intentional infliction of mental or emotional distress is defined by extreme and outrageous conduct of severe emotional or mental distress even in the absence of physical harm. The Defendant desired to cause the Plaintiff emotional distress because Thomas Norkus knew if she discovered the affair she would be devastated and knew with substantial certainty that plaintiff would suffer severe emotional distress and recklessly disregarded the high probability that severe emotional distress would occur.

Analysis: Dr. Fisher discovered the affair on the security cameras in the home of Dr. Fisher and Dr. Norkus. When Dr. Fisher confronted Dr. Norkus he stated she would not have discovered the affair if she did not have the security cameras. Dr. Norkus knew about Dr. Fisher being super sensitive because of family and business partners lying to her and using her in the past. Dr. Fisher is now on 2 types of blood pressure medicine and a medication for post traumatic distress disorder. She is on Atenolol and Valsartan for her blood pressure and fluvoxamine for her post traumatic stress disorder.

Conclusion: Thomas Norkus caused Dr. Fisher severe emotional and mental distress and owes Dr. Fisher punitive damages due to the severe mental and emotional distress caused when by the fact that she caught them on the security camera at Dr. Fisher and Thomas Norkus' home was outrageous. The actions of Thomas Norkus against Dr. Fisher is the proximate cause of the severe emotional and mental distress that Dr. Fisher suffered. Thomas Norkus knew that Dr. Fisher was a very sensitive person in the area of being used and lied to because of Dr. Fisher's being used and lied to by her mother and business partners. The case in question against her ex business partners is 13-CVS-579. Thomas Norkus was with Dr. Fisher at her bankruptcy hearing that was caused by John and Carl Whaley. Thomas Norkus new everything but he did not care. He decided to use her and lie to her anyway. Dr. Fisher believes Thomas Norkus owes her compensatory damages in excess of

$15000.00 and punitive damages because of the severe mental and emotional distress suffered at the behavior of Thomas Norkus. Dr. Fisher did not have to go on blood pressure medicine until the stress she was put under because of Thomas Norkus and she had to go back on fluvoxamine because of the stress caused by Thomas Norkus. Dr. Fisher has suffered both financial and physical harm because of the behavior of Thomas Norkus toward her. Thomas Norkus also knows how religious Dr. Fisher is. Their first date was at a Eucharistic convention in Charlotte in September 2013. Also, both Dr. Fisher and Thomas Norkus are Catholic. Thomas Norkus willfully caused the emotional distress because he knew the high probability of the emotional distress would suffer if she caught him cheating on her.

Issue: Was Dr. Norkus involved in a criminal conspiracy to commit a crime and that resulted in harming Dr. Fisher financially, mentally, and emotionally?
Rule: When there are 2 or more persons involved and an unlawful objective to be achieved, an agreement as to the means to achieve objective, and one or more overt acts in furtherance of the conspiracy, and a resulting injury or damages occurred.
Analysis: There were 3 people involved in the fraud and cover-up of the adulterous affair between Mrs. Williams and Thomas Norkus. William Joe Goodman helped Thomas Norkus hide the affair from Dr. Fisher between Mrs. Williams and Thomas Norkus. William Joe Goodman was a roommate of Dr. Fisher and Thomas Norkus who moved in Feb. 2014 but was evicted in September 2014 by Thomas Norkus because he was arrested and put in jail due to various charges. The unlawful objective of Thomas Norkus, Emily Williams, and William Joe Goodman was to hide the adulterous affair between Thomas Norkus and Emily Williams so Dr. Fisher would not leave. Thomas Norkus did not want to lose Dr. Fisher's money. Fraud and adultery are illegal in North Carolina.
Conclusion: There was a criminal conspiracy between Thomas Norkus, Emily Williams, and William Joe Goodman to hide the adulterous affair between Thomas Norkus and Emily Williams. Dr.

Fisher suffered financial harm and extreme emotional and mental distress. Dr. Fisher should be allowed to receive compensatory damages and punitive damages from Thomas Norkus. Thomas Norkus is jointly and severally liable for the compensatory and punitive damages owed to Dr. Fisher. The criminal conspiracy that occurred between Thomas Norkus, Emily Williams, and William Joe Goodman is the proximate cause of the financial harm and extreme emotional and mental distress caused to Dr. Fisher. The amount of money that Dr. Fisher lost was over $15000.00 so the fraud involved is considered a felony. There are no statute of limitations on felonies in NC. Adultery is a Class 2 misdemeanor for both parties involved and can involve both fines and jail time.

Emily Williams

She is an instructor at Belmont Abbey College in the English Department. She is married to a Mr. David Morris Williams. Her adulterous relationship with Thomas Norkus interfered with the enjoyment of Dr. Fisher's enjoyment of her home when Dr. Fisher discovered Mrs. Williams was in an adulterous relationship with Thomas Norkus. Dr. Fisher and Thomas Norkus were dating when Dr. Fisher found out about the adulterous relationship between Mrs. Williams and Thomas Norkus. Emily Williams agreed to meet Thomas Norkus in private at the home of Dr. Fisher and Thomas Norkus when Dr. Fisher was not at home. Mrs. Williams' actions proved that she conspired with Dr. Norkus to keep the adulterous relationship hidden from Dr. Fisher. She caused Dr. Fisher severe mental and emotional distress. This conduct was outrageous. Mrs. Williams' husband is 48 years old and still lives with Mrs. Williams. The name of Mrs. Emily Williams' husband is David Williams and he is a professor at Belmont Abbey College and a Dean at Belmont Abbey College.

Issue: Is Mrs. Emily Williams guilty of fraud and conspiracy to commit fraud because Mrs. Williams helped   Thomas Norkus and William Joe Goodman to hide the adulterous affair with she was having with Thomas Norkus from Dr. Fisher?

Rule: A person that helps another person benefit from a misrepresentation of a material fact and/or benefits himself or herself from helping another person is guilty of fraud

Analysis: Mrs. Williams helped Dr. Norkus hide the adulterous affair between them so Dr. Fisher would continue to pay for household repairs and/or upgrades and for the dates between Dr. Fisher and Dr. Norkus and so Dr. Fisher would not move out. Mrs. Williams owed a duty to Dr. Fisher because Dr. Fisher was a foreseeable victim in Mrs. Williams' affair with Dr. Norkus.

Conclusion: Mrs. Williams benefited from the affair because Dr. Norkus gave her jewelry and she had access to all the sundries and groceries Dr. Fisher bought for the household. Dr. Fisher did not give Mrs. Williams' permission to access anything that Dr. Fisher bought for the home of Dr. Fisher and Thomas Norkus. In conclusion, Mrs. Williams committed fraud and the conspiracy to commit fraud with Dr. Thomas Norkus and William Joe Goodman. Mrs. Williams is jointly and severally for the fraud suffered by Dr. Fisher because of the adulterous affair Mrs. Williams had with Dr. Norkus. Mrs. Williams' had a duty to Dr. Fisher to make sure that the relationship between Dr. Norkus and Mrs. Williams did not damage Dr. Fisher. Mrs. Williams did not use a reasonable amount of care in her duty to Dr. Fisher. Mrs. Williams' fraud and conspiracy to commit fraud with Thomas Norkus is a proximate cause of the financial harm caused to Dr. Fisher. As well as the emotional and mental distress Dr. Fisher suffered.

Issue: Did Mrs. Williams' adulterous affair with Thomas Norkus cause Dr. Fisher negligent and intentional severe emotional and mental distress when Dr. Fisher discovered the affair?

Rule: The torts of negligent and intentional infliction of mental or emotional distress is defined by extreme and outrageous conduct of severe emotional or mental distress even in the absence of physical harm. The Defendant desired to cause the Plaintiff emotional distress if she discovered the affair and knew with substantial certainty that plaintiff would suffer emotional distress and recklessly disregarded the high probability that emotional distress would occur.

Analysis: Any woman married or not should know someone cheating with her boyfriend in her own home would cause the woman severe and emotional distress. Mrs. Williams has proven that she does not care about anyone but herself because she agreed to meet Thomas Norkus in private and kept the affair hidden from Dr. Fisher. She willfully caused Dr. Fisher's emotional distress because she acted in disregard of the high probability that Dr. Fisher would suffer emotional distress if she found out about the adultery.

Conclusion: Mrs. Williams is jointly and severally liable for the compensatory damages and punitive damages due to Dr. Fisher because she was responsible for helping to cause Dr. Fisher severe negligent and intentional emotional distress because of Mrs. Williams' affair with Thomas Norkus. Mrs. Williams did not use a reasonable amount of care to make sure that Dr. Fisher was not harmed in any way by the affair between Mrs. Williams and Thomas Norkus. Mrs. Williams was a proximate cause that was responsible for Dr. Fisher's negligent and intentional emotional distress. Mrs. Williams also broke her marriage vows with David Williams, her husband.

William Joe Goodman:
Issue: Did Joe Williams commit fraud against Dr. Fisher by helping Dr. Norkus and Emily Williams cover up their adulterous affair? Rule: An intent to induce the plaintiff's reliance on the misrepresentation.

Analysis: William Joe Goodman was aware that there was an adulterous affair going on between Emily Williams and Thomas Norkus and never told Dr. Fisher that an affair was going until he came back from jail. William Joe Goodman was a roommate of Dr. Fisher and Thomas Norkus. Thomas Norkus evicted Joe and when Joe got out of jail and came back to 516 Northgate Ave, he then proceeded to tell Dr. Fisher that Thomas Norkus has been seeing Emily Williams behind Dr. Fisher's back.   Dr. Fisher did not believe

William Joe Goodman at that time because he was being extremely spiteful. He was so spiteful that Dr. Fisher became scared and moved to a motel after work in the middle of the night and would not come back until Thomas Norkus had William Joe Goodman out of the house.

Conclusion: William Joe Goodman is jointly and several liable for the compensatory damages due to Dr. Fisher because of the fraud committed against Dr. Fisher because he helped cover-up the adultery, and benefitted from the cover-up. He committed fraud against Dr. Fisher by his own actions.

Issue: Did William Joe Goodman cause Dr. Fisher extreme emotional and mental distress from his statement to her after he came home from jail and helping Thomas Norkus conduct an adulterous affair which he helped keep hidden from Dr. Fisher because it benefitted him to do that?

Rule: The tort of intentional infliction of mental and/or emotional distress is defined by extreme and outrageous conduct of severe emotional or mental distress even in the absence of physical harm.

Analysis: Dr. Fisher suffered severe emotional and mental distress from the spiteful words Joe said to her when he came home from jail in August 2014. That is why she left in the middle of the night and cut him off totally. He scared her and so she left when he was asleep. She left Thomas Norkus to handle Joe. His conduct was extreme and outrageous and he desired to cause Dr. Fisher emotional distress and recklessly disregarded the high probability that emotional and mental distress would occur.

Conclusion: William Joe Goodman is jointly and severally liable for the compensatory and punitive damages that Dr. Fisher is requesting due to extreme emotional and mental distress. William Joe Goodman was very spiteful when he returned to 516 Northgate Ave from jail and he did not care how much emotional distress he caused Dr. Fisher. He wanted to hurt her because Thomas Norkus was evicting him and Dr. Fisher and Thomas Norkus refused to bail him out of jail.

Issue: Was William Joe Goodman involved in a criminal conspiracy to fraud Dr. Fisher and cause her extreme emotional and mental distress?

Rule: When there are 2 or more persons involved and an unlawful objective to be achieved, an agreement as to the means to achieve objective, and one or more overt acts in furtherance of the conspiracy, and a resulting injury or damages occurred.

Analysis: William Joe Goodman helped Thomas Norkus and Emily Williams hide the adulterous affair between Thomas Norkus and Emily Williams because he benefitted from it financially. William Joe Goodman benefitted from the adulterous affair between Thomas Norkus and Emily Williams because Thomas Norkus let him slide a lot on the rent.

Conclusion: William Joe Goodman conspired with Thomas Norkus and Emily Williams to commit fraud against Dr. Fisher and cause her extreme emotional and mental distress. He also extorted money from Dr. Fisher to get him out of the home belonging to Dr. Fisher and Dr. Norkus. Dr. Fisher has proof of everything. William Joe Goodman also committed assault and battery against Dr. Fisher when he pinched Dr. Fisher. It was a pinch like someone who deliberately wanted to cause someone else extreme pain.

David M. Williams:

Issue: Did David Williams know about the adulterous affair between Thomas Norkus and his wife Mrs. Emily Williams

Rule: When there are 2 or more persons involved and an unlawful objective to be achieved, an agreement as to the means to achieve objective, and one or more overt acts in furtherance of the conspiracy, and a resulting injury or damages occurred.

Anaylsis: If David Williams knew about the adulterous relationship between Thomas Norkus and his wife Emily Williams he is part of the conspiracy and is guilty as all the other parties in this complaint. He then should be added to every part of the complaint. Thomas Norkus told Dr. Fisher when she confronted him that David Williams knew about the affair but did not care. Dr. Fisher told Thomas Norkus that she did not care about the relationship between David

Williams and his wife Emily Williams except for the fact it disrupted her life and hurt her because of her relationship with Thomas Norkus.

Conclusion: If it is shown that David Williams knew about the adulterous relationship between Thomas Norkus and his wife Emily Williams, he is as guilty as all the other parties in this complaint and should be added to the complaint. Dr. Fisher wants an injunction to apply to Mr. David Williams regardless of whether he knew or not. The injunction is to cease any form of contact between Thomas Norkus and William Joe Goodman and himself. Dr. Fisher does not believe he knew anything but she wants to cover all her bases.

The Background of Dr. Fisher, Thomas Norkus, Emily Williams, and William Joe Goodman

Dr. Fisher wanted to make sure the court received the full story, so they will know that this was more than personal.

Thomas Norkus is a pharmacist with Cardinal Health and Dr. Fisher is a traveling pharmacist with Walgreens. Dr. Fisher dated Thomas Norkus from 2012 thru September 2014.

Thomas Norkus committed fraud against Dr. Fisher because he failed to inform Dr. Fisher while they were dating that he became involved in an adulterous relationship with Emily Williams. Dr. Fisher paid for all of their dates and put money into what she then considered their house. If Dr. Fisher had known about the adulterous relationship Dr. Fisher would have moved out before the adulterous relationship started. Dr. Fisher discovered the relationship when she and Thomas Norkus had security cameras installed in the house and caught Mrs. Williams at their house in the kitchen and living room with Thomas Norkus. Dr. Fisher told Thomas Norkus before she caught him cheating that she would move out if he wanted to start dating other people. Both Dr. Fisher and Thomas Norkus are Catholic. Dr. Fisher used to be a Baptist but became a Catholic in April 2012 before Thomas Norkus and Dr. Fisher started dating. Dr. Fisher did move in with Tom in January 2014 but never shared his bed because she made a vow several years ago to not share a man's bed again unless she married him.

Thomas Norkus agreed to that because Thomas Norkus and Dr. Fisher started dating. Also, Thomas Norkus allowed Dr. Fisher to put him on her checking account while he was in an adulterous relationship with Emily Williams. Dr. Fisher wanted to show Thomas Norkus that she trusted him is the reason she put him on her checking account. As soon as she found out about the adulterous affair with Emily Williams, she had Thomas Norkus taken off her checking account. She has never really trusted him again. Thomas Norkus is almost 10 years older than Dr. Fisher and almost 26 years older than Mrs. Williams. Dr. Fisher spent in excess of $15,000 on Thomas Norkus and their home in 2014 while Dr. Fisher was living with him that year. Dr. Fisher officially moved from Charlotte in December 2014 to Shelby NC. Dr. Fisher is originally from Shelby NC. Thomas Norkus kept Dr. Fisher from moving when he told he would move instead to Cary NC probably because that is where he works at. According to the last phone conversation between Dr. Fisher and Thomas Norkus; Thomas Norkus told Dr. Fisher he wanted to make things right and wanted to be Dr. Fisher's friend again. She thought he meant by paying her back the rest of the money she spent on him and his house in 2014. Thomas Norkus came to Shelby twice to return stuff to Dr. Fisher and write Dr. Fisher a check for a portion of what he owed her. And to get the security system switched to her name.

When Dr. Fisher discovered that Thomas Norkus was cheating on her it was devastating because of everything Dr. Fisher has been thru in the last few years. Dr. Fisher never thought Thomas Norkus would actually cheat on her nor use her or lie to her because he knew how extremely sensitive Dr. Fisher was because of people using her and lying to her in her past. Her own mother was one of those people. So were her business partners Carl and John Whaley. Dr. Fisher had to declare bankruptcy and allow her bankruptcy trustee to settle the civil side against Carl and John Whaley. Tom knew everything, Tom even went to Dr. Fisher's bankruptcy hearing with her and held her hand until they called her case. Tom Norkus used Dr. Fisher for her money while he was cheating on her. If he had told Dr. Fisher he wanted to see other people she would have moved out and cut him out of her life entirely. Dr. Fisher would have eventually forgiven him for the cheating but the lying to her and using her for her money is something she has a major problem with. Dr. Fisher was gradually getting over her trust issues but not anymore. She has major trust issues again.

He had an issue with the Board of Pharmacy when he tried to open his own pharmacy thru fraud. He almost lost his license. Dr. Fisher supported him and helped him find an attorney when he had to go before the board. He almost lost his pharmacy license because of his actions in trying to open his own pharmacy. The SC Board of Pharmacy put him on probation because of his NC Board of Pharmacy issue.

Thomas Norkus has a habit of committing fraud against people and/or corporations. Dr. Fisher thought he could change but she was wrong! Dr. Fisher is enclosing the proof of the NC and SC Board reprimands. Dr. Fisher also put Thomas Norkus on her bank account but took him off her bank account when she found out he was cheating on her. Thomas Norkus committed fraud against NC Mutual Drug by sending drugs back which he did not have the pedigrees for in order to get money from NC Mutual Drug to be able to start his own pharmacy. It was over a $1000 worth of drugs he sent back to get money, so this is a Class H felony. There are no statute of limitations in NC on felonies. Which means that he can still be prosecuted on the fraud committed against NC Mutual Drug. Dr. Fisher is enclosing the issues with the NC and SC Boards of Pharmacy to prove that Thomas Norkus is not an honest person and has a habit of committing fraud against people and/or corporations. Dr. Fisher has told him on several occasions that she would give him a second chance if he started to make things right and started acting right. She was planning on giving him another chance until she discovered he was still seeing Mrs. Williams. She also tried to call him about some stuff she ordered thru Amazon that went to his place accidently. He refused to answer Dr. Fisher calls about the merchandise but eventually sent her stuff one day delivery to her in Shelby, NC when she told him that she would not give him another chance.

Thomas Norkus has reimbursed Dr. Fisher almost $3500 so far for what she spent on him and his house in 2014. However, he also took tiles from Dr. Fisher's old house right before he told her he decided not to move to Cary. Dr. Fisher had already told Thomas Norkus that if he did not move out she would. Even during that conversation he told Dr. Fisher to take her time and that he could never live in Shelby, NC. Of course as soon as he told her that she knew she was going to move to Shelby, NC. Dr. Fisher would have moved out before Thomas Norkus started the adulterous relationship if she had known. Dr. Fisher found a place in Shelby, NC and moved out. Dr. Norkus took ceramic tiles from Dr. Fisher's old house. She has requested those tiles back or reimbursement for those tiles. He also took her father's tools from her old house but he brought those back. Dr. Fisher is also requesting reimbursement for the 3 weeks she had to stay in a motel while he got William Joe Goodman out of the house.

William Joe Goodman or Joe as he was called became a roommate of Dr. Fisher and Thomas Norkus in February 2014. Dr. Fisher did not know he was moving in until he actually moved in. Dr. Fisher told Tom that she did not trust Joe on several occasions. Joe was late on his rent and utilities as soon as he moved in. He never became caught up on any of his bills. Dr. Fisher thinks Joe started blackmailing Tom about his adulterous relationship with Emily Williams at some point in April 2014 because that is when he stopped keeping up with what Joe owed him. Dr. Fisher kept up with everything though. Dr. Fisher now realizes it was probably blackmail because Thomas Norkus did not want Dr. Fisher to leave. He kept her from leaving when Joe wound up in jail because she left and went to a motel for 3 weeks until Thomas Norkus got William Joe Goodman moved out. Dr. Fisher told Thomas Norkus that unless he got Joe out she would not move back. Thomas Norkus got Joe out. Joe extorted $750.00 from Dr. Fisher and Thomas Norkus before he would move out. Dr. Fisher paid that money. Well Dr. Fisher gave the money to Thomas Norkus to give to Joe, so that he would move out quicker.

Praying for relief from the court:

An injunction that stops Thomas Norkus, Emily Williams, and Williams Joe Goodman from ever meeting or congregating or having any contact with each other again because of the financial harm caused to Dr. Fisher because of the relationship between these 3 people. Also because of the severe mental and emotional distress Dr. Fisher suffered because of the relationship between Thomas Norkus, Emily Williams and William Joe Goodman. Dr. Fisher was not the only person hurt in this situation. Dr. David Williams was also hurt because of the adulterous relationship between Emily Williams and Thomas Norkus. Mr. David Williams is the husband of Mrs. Emily Williams. I also want the injunction to include that Mr. David Williams cannot meet or contact in any form Thomas Norkus or William Joe Goodman ever.

If it pleases the court, Dr. Fisher would like to be paid back all the money she spent on Thomas Norkus and his house in 2014. The money Dr. Fisher spent was in excess of 15,000. Dr. Fisher did try to get in touch with Mr. Norkus to work out a settlement between them but Thomas Norkus told Dr. Fisher to never get in touch with him again, so she had no choice but to go thru the courts. Dr. Fisher is requesting that he pay for all meals she purchased for him in 2014 and half of the groceries and the house cleaning she had done. And reimburse her for any money she spent on his house that he has not already reimbursed her for. She is requesting this because if she had been told by Thomas Norkus that he was wanting to date other people before he started an adulterous relationship with Emily Williams she would have moved out long before she did. Dr. Fisher does not condone adultery of any kind. Thomas Norkus knew what Dr. Fisher had been thru and was still going thru but he lied to her and used her anyway. Emily Williams and William Joe Goodman helped Thomas Norkus deceive Dr. Fisher, so she would continue spending money on Thomas Norkus and his house.

Dr. Fisher does believe she deserves punitive damages because of what she had to go thru in 2014 because of the relationship between Thomas Norkus, Emily Williams, and William Joe Goodman. However, Dr. Fisher just wants to be reimbursed totally for all the money that she spent on Thomas Norkus and his house in 2014 from Thomas Norkus and a permanent injunction of Thomas Norkus, Emily Williams, and Joe Goodman from ever having any form of contact with each other again. Dr. Fisher would like to include David Williams in in an injunction from ever having contact with Thomas Norkus and William Joe Goodman because he is the husband of Emily Williams. Dr. Fisher would not support the lifestyle of an adulterer knowingly. Adultery offends Dr. Fisher greatly because of her religious beliefs.

Adultery is illegal in North Carolina. Thomas Norkus admitted to Dr. Fisher that he was having an affair with Mrs. Williams when she confronted him after catching him and Mrs. Emily Williams together with the security camera in their house.

The house that Dr. Fisher and Thomas Norkus was living in Charlotte, NC. Dr. Fisher now lives in Shelby NC. She moved back to Shelby in December 2014.

Thomas Norkus gained financially from Dr. Fisher by hiding the adulterous affair he had with Mrs. Williams from Dr. Fisher. Mrs. Wiliams gained financially from Thomas Norkus in the form of jewelry from Thomas Norkus when Mrs. Williams helped Thomas Norkus hide her adulterous affair with him. Dr. Fisher is making an educated guess that the jewelry that Thomas Norkus gave Mrs. Williams was for sexual services she rendered to him also. William Joe Goodman blackmailed Thomas Norkus in the form of not paying much rent and extortion against Dr. Fisher and Thomas Norkus when Thomas Norkus evicted William Joe Goodman. When Thomas Norkus finally was able to get Joe moved out, Joe owed Mr. Norkus at least $3000.00.

If Thomas Norkus is not willing to work out a settlement with Dr. Fisher. Dr. Fisher is asking the court for a jury trial. Dr. Fisher does not know what kind of arrangement that David Williams and his wife Emily Williams has. However, Dr. Fisher does know that the dysfunctional marriage between David Williams and his wife did effect Dr. Fisher because of the affair that occurred between Thomas Norkus and Emily Williams. I am praying for both David Williams and his wife. I do not believe in divorce and I pray that David Williams and his wife are able to work things out. I am also praying that Thomas Norkus starts doing what is correct in the eyes of the Lord. If David Williams knew about the affair between Thomas Norkus and his wife, she would like the court's permission to add David Williams to the complaint. Dr. Fisher believes spousal privilege is barred in this complaint because Emily Williams is guilty of crimes in NC that involve a criminal conspiracy against a third party. Mrs. Williams has been accused of fraud against Dr. Fisher because she helped Thomas Norkus hide the adulterous affair between Thomas Norkus and herself and she gained financially in the affair with Thomas Norkus. Dr. Fisher did suffer financially because she did not know that Thomas Norkus was involved in an adulterous affair. Thomas Norkus, Emily Williams, and William Joe Goodman all gained financially.

Dr. Fisher does want the court to know that she was and is offended greatly by anyone committing adultery. She does consider herself a Christian and she knows she is not better than anyone else. However, finding out that Thomas Norkus was engaged in an adulterous affair (cheating on her) behind her back caused her extreme emotional and mental distress because Dr. Fisher and Thomas Norkus were dating and she spent a lot of money on Thomas Norkus and his house at 516 Northgate Ave in Charlotte NC. He has given Dr. Fisher some of the money back she spent on him and his house in 2014 but not all of it. He has stated he wants to make it right and the only way to do that is to reimburse her for everything she spent on him and his house last year. She also wants to be reimbursed for moving expenses and medical expenses because of the blood pressure medicine and anxiety medicine Dr. Fisher had to go on because of Thomas Norkus. Dr. Fisher wants to be reimbursed for all legal expenses because she was willing to work out a settlement with him. After Dr. Fisher told him that she be would be willing to work out a settlement, he told her not to contact him again or it would be considered harassment. The only reason Dr. Fisher moved out was because she caught him cheating on her. Dr. Fisher would not have spent anything on Thomas Norkus or his house if she had known he was cheating on her. All he had to do was tell her he wanted to start dating other people before he started an adulterous relationship and she would have moved out and cut him totally out of her life then. Dr. Fisher and Thomas Norkus were living together but not sharing a bed because she is not willing to share a bed with a man unless she is married to him. Dr. Fisher told Thomas Norkus that she would not share his bed unless she married him. He agreed to that so they started dating. Thomas Norkus has told Dr. Fisher on several occasion that she is a strong willed woman. The only reason she considers herself a strong willed is because she is a woman that says yes to the Lord.

If at all possible Dr. Fisher would love the court to require both Thomas Norkus and Emily Williams' to pay fines for committing adultery and make each of them serve 60 days in jail, the minimum jail time for adultery in North Carolina. Of course Dr. Fisher knows this is civil court so that might be outside of this court's jurisdiction. Dr. Fisher believes that Thomas Norkus has not learned his lesson when he almost lost his pharmacy license in 2 different states because he committed fraud against NC Mutual Drug. He committed fraud against Dr. Fisher after she moved in with him. Thomas Norkus has always encouraged Dr. Fisher to use the law to obtain justice against the parties that have wronged her. This time Thomas Norkus is one of those parties. She is praying that she is using the law correctly and for justice.

If Dr. Fisher has stated or done anything incorrectly she prays that the court will allow her to correct any mistake or the licensed attorney she plans to retain to help settle this complaint. Dr. Fisher is also apologizing for her emotional state because she was severely hurt by the adultery, fraud, blackmail, and extortion that has caused this complaint.

To The Best of Dr. Cynthia Ann Fisher's knowledge everything is true as stated in this complaint and she is certifying each copy before a notary republic.

Date_____

Plaintiff
signature:_____

Dr. Cynthia A. Fisher

Vs.

David and Emily
Williams

Opposition to Motion to Dismiss and Amended Complaint with Memorandum of Law

Dr. Fisher is amending the complaint against Mrs. William only. Dr. Fisher would like to add the tort of trespass and private nuisance against Mrs. Williams. Mrs. Wiliams was in Dr. Fisher's without Dr. Fisher's permission. That is trespass. Any food or drink in the household in Charlotte, NC was purchased by Dr. Fisher. Any item consumed by Mrs. Williams would constitute theft because she did not have Dr. Fisher's permission to consume anything purchased by Dr. Fisher. Dr. Fisher believes Mrs. Williams was allowed in Dr. Fisher's car. Mrs. Williams never had Dr. Fisher's permission to ride in her car. That is trespass also.

Mrs. Williams adulterous relationship with Thomas Norkus was both a public and private nuisance because adultery is a major sin. It is against one of the 10 commandments in both the Catholic Bible and the King James Version. Adultery is an act against the moral fiber of the community and therefore is a public nuisance.

Dr. Fisher had a possessory interest in the home located at 516 Northgate Ave, Charlotte NC because of the amount of money she spent on the home while she was living there. Mrs. Williams was having an adulterous relationship with Dr. Fisher's boyfriend in Dr. Fisher's own home. That is definitely a private nuisance. Dr. Fisher did not give her permission to have an adulterous relationship with her boyfriend. Thomas Norkus was Dr. Fisher's boyfriend at the time the adulterous relationship occurred in her home.

Mrs. Williams committed adultery with Thomas Norkus in the house of Dr. Fisher and Thomas Norkus. Dr. Fisher and Thomas Norkus were sharing a house but not a bed because of the religious beliefs of Dr. Fisher. Dr. Fisher and Thomas Norkus are not married. However Emily Williams is married to David Williams. Adultery is against the law for both parties involved and it does not matter which party is involved. Under North Carolina General Statute section 14-84. In NC a person or persons committing adultery may be subject to 60 days of active punishment or $1000 fine or both. Adultery is considered a class 2 misdemeanor and is subject to active, intermediate, or community punishment and/or fines depending on prior convictions.

Thomas Norkus has settled with Dr. Fisher out of court for himself only. He has also apologized to Dr. Fisher for hurting her. Mr. Norkus admitted to Dr. Fisher that he was in an adulterous relationship with Emily Williams after Dr. Fisher caught him with her at their house with their security cameras.

Furthermore, neither David Williams nor his wife Emily Williams have denied anything in their answer to the complaint against them. By not denying anything they admitted to everything. Including criminal fraud and conspiracy. The amount of money Dr. Fisher lost was in excess of $15,000 because of the adulterous relationship between Thomas Norkus and Emily Williams. The fraud committed against Dr. Fisher is a class H felony. And criminal conspiracy is a class I felony for this type of crime. There are no statutes of limitations for felonies in North Carolina.

Fraud occurs when someone deceives a person and gains something of value from that person.

Conspiracy to commit fraud is when 2 or more people are involved in a cover up.

Dr. Fisher was devastated emotionally and mentally. And offended greatly when she discovered the adulterous relationship between Thomas Norkus and Emily Williams. First because Dr. Fisher and Thomas Norkus were dating. And she was greatly offended because of her religious beliefs. Dr. Fisher is a Catholic and she goes to church at St. Mary's in Shelby, NC. Thomas Norkus is a Catholic also but he is excommunicated because of his adulterous actions.

Dr. Fisher had to see a medical doctor because of the stress and posttraumatic stress syndrome that Dr. Fisher experienced because of this entire situation. Dr. Fisher is now on 2 blood pressure medications and a medication used for posttraumatic stress.

Dr. Fisher would have been willing to marry Thomas Norkus until she discovered him cheating on her. Dr. Fisher and Thomas did discuss marriage before they started dating. Dr. Fisher let Thomas Norkus know that she would not share a bed with him unless she married him. Thomas Norkus agreed to those terms.

Marriage is a contract between 2 people. Mrs. Williams interfered with a prospective marriage contract between Dr. Fisher and Thomas Norkus.

Negligent and Intentional mental and emotional distress

Case law concerning adultery and emotional distress

Dr. Fisher is praying to the court not to dismiss this case because of the civil, criminal, and moral issues involved. Dr. Fisher is praying to the court for a jury trial concerning the issues involved. Dr. Fisher is seeking compensatory damages and injunctions for the damage that occurred to her life as a result of Mrs. Emily William having an adulterous relationship in Dr. Fisher's home without Dr. Fisher's knowledge. The dysfunctional marriage between David Williams and his wife Emily Williams harmed Dr. Fisher's life and David Williams never denied the fact that he knew the adulterous relationship with Thomas Norkus was taking place between Thomas Norkus and his wife and by not denying he knew, he was admitting he knew. Which makes David Williams as guilty as his wife.

If David Williams did not know he can go after Thomas Norkus legally for Alienation of Affection or Criminal Conversation in the civil courts.

Dr. Fisher is praying to the court for David Williams and Mrs. Williams to compensate her for the difference which Thomas Norkus did not compensate Dr. Fisher for and Dr. Fisher can prove all amounts to the court.

Mrs. Williams is considered a principal in the first degree because Mrs. Williams conspired with Thomas Norkus to keep the adulterous affair between Thomas Norkus and Mrs. Williams so Thomas Norkus could continue to benefit financially because Dr. Fisher was living with Thomas Norkus. Dr. Fisher invested quite a bit of money into Thomas Norkus and their relationship. Including work on their home in Charlotte, NC.

The punitive damages that Dr. Fisher is praying for from the court is 2 letters of apology from David Williams and his wife Emily Williams for their selfish acts that created havoc in Dr. Fisher's life.

Dr. Fisher is also praying to the court for any other compensation or punitive damages the court deems appropriate. Dr. Fisher plans to have the help of a licensed attorney at trial or in any settlement conference.

Dr. Fisher admits that she is extremely upset because of this situation. Dr. Fisher was harmed financially and emotionally because of the adulterous relationship which occurred between Mrs. Williams and Thomas Norkus, Dr. Fisher's boyfriend at the time the adulterous relationship took place. Dr. Fisher was also morally and religiously offended by the conduct that took place in her own home.

In the General Court of Jurisdiction
Superior Court Division
15 CVS 610

Dr. Cynthia A. Fisher

Vs.

David and Emily
Williams

Opposition to Motion to Dismiss and Memorandum of Law

The dysfunctional relationship between Emily Williams and her husband David Williams resulted in an adulterous relationship between Thomas Norkus and Emily Williams. This adulterous relationship affected my life because I was dating Thomas Norkus when he became involved in an adulterous relationship with Emily Williams. I left Thomas Norkus when I discovered the adulterous relationship between Thomas Norkus and Emily Williams.

Actually, one of the main issues, I think will survive is that the dysfunctional relationship between David Williams and Emily Williams impacted my life and should not have. It is true that this court does not handle criminal cases. However, I am asking for injunctions because of the criminal law at issue here.

I know I am thinking outside the box but this is a question concerning how the dysfunctional marriage between Emily and David Williams affected my life and why it affected my life. I think this is a unique take on an old situation. Adultery is both a crime and a moral sin. Which is why I think a jury should be allowed to decide this case.

Another reason I think motion to dismiss is being asserted is that both David Williams and his wife Emily Williams work at Belmont Abbey College. David Williams is Vice President of Academic Affairs and Dean of the faculty at Belmont Abbey College. Emily Williams is an instructor in English at Belmont Abbey College.

I did want to let the court know I am a Catholic also. I attend St. Mary's here in Shelby, NC.

Also, from what I understand the elements of the tort actions do not have to be stated in the initial complaint because we are in the pre-litigation stages. I also realized that some of my tort claims will not survive until the trial. However, this not the trial. Also, there is a lot of overlap between tort issues and criminal issues. That is why I am in the process of getting the criminal issues investigated by the fraud and financial crimes unit at CMPD.

Thomas Norkus was my boyfriend but I left him when I found out he was having an adulterous relationship with Emily Williams. I know that Mr. Arnold sent a memorandum of law in support of the motion to dismiss.

I did not know that Thomas Norkus had given her permission to be at our house without her husband present and he should not have. I did not find this out until I caught them together at my house on my security tape.

I have received a notice of hearing but before I received the notice of hearing I sent Mr. and Mrs. Williams requests for admissions. Their attorney was to get an extension of time to answer said admissions thru October 28, 2015. Dr. Fisher believes that the hearing for the motion to dismiss should be postponed until she received the answers to the admissions she requests. And Dr. Fisher is opposing the motion to dismiss with a memorandum of law.

Mrs. Williams' adulterous relationship with Thomas Norkus was both a public and private nuisance because adultery is a major sin. It is against one of the 10 commandments in both the Catholic Bible and the King James Version. Adultery is an act against the moral fiber of the community and therefore is a public nuisance.

Dr. Fisher had a possessory interest in the home located at 516 Northgate Ave, Charlotte NC because of the amount of money she spent on the home while she was living there. Mrs. Williams was having an adulterous relationship with Dr. Fisher's boyfriend in Dr. Fisher's own home. That is definitely a private nuisance. Dr. Fisher did not give her permission to have an adulterous relationship with her boyfriend. Thomas Norkus was Dr. Fisher's boyfriend at the time the adulterous relationship occurred in her home.

Mrs. Williams committed adultery with Thomas Norkus in the house of Dr. Fisher and Thomas Norkus. Dr. Fisher and Thomas Norkus were sharing a house but not a bed because of the religious beliefs of Dr. Fisher. Dr. Fisher and Thomas Norkus are not married.

However Emily Williams is married to David Williams. Adultery is against the law for both parties involved in North Carolina and it does not matter which party involved is married. Under North Carolina General Statute section 14-84. In NC a person or persons committing adultery may be subject to 60 days of active punishment or $1000 fine or both. Adultery is considered a class 2 misdemeanor and is subject to active, intermediate, or community punishment and/or fines depending on prior convictions.

Thomas Norkus has settled with Dr. Fisher out of court for himself only. He has also apologized to Dr. Fisher for hurting her. Mr. Norkus admitted to Dr. Fisher that he was in an adulterous relationship with Emily Williams after Dr. Fisher caught him with her at their house with their security cameras.

Furthermore, neither David Williams nor his wife Emily Williams have denied anything in their answer to the complaint against them. By not denying anything they admitted to everything. Including criminal fraud and conspiracy. The amount of money Dr. Fisher lost was in excess of $15,000 because of the adulterous relationship between Thomas Norkus and Emily Williams. The fraud committed against Dr. Fisher is a class H felony. And criminal conspiracy is a class I felony for this type of crime. There are no statutes of limitations for felonies in North Carolina.

Fraud (common law deceit) occurs when someone deceives a person and gains something of value from that person. Thomas Norkus gained money and food from Dr. Fisher because she relied on the fact that he was not cheating on her. Mrs. Williams conspired with Thomas Norkus to keep the cheating adulterous affair from Dr. Fisher. Because she was an accomplice in Thomas Norkus cover up of a crime that was taking place in Dr. Fisher's home, she is guilty of the fraud. Adultery is a crime also and is the original crime that was hidden from Dr. Fisher.

Conspiracy to commit fraud is when 2 or more people are involved in a cover up. The people in the criminal cover up are considered accomplices and they are liable for crimes they did or counsel and for any other foreseeable crimes committed in the course of committing the crime to the same extent as the principal. Mrs. Williams is just as guilty as Tom based on the NC definitions. Mr. Williams is guilty also because he did not deny that he knew about the adulterous affair that was taking place between Thomas Norkus and Mrs. Williams, which makes Mr. Williams an accomplice also

The fraud committed in this situation is considered a class H felony and the conspiracy to commit fraud is a class I felony if I am understanding the crime classification in NC. I think I am.

Dr. Fisher was devastated emotionally and mentally. And offended greatly when she discovered the adulterous relationship between Thomas Norkus and Emily Williams. First because Dr. Fisher and Thomas Norkus were dating. And she was greatly offended because of her religious beliefs. Dr. Fisher is a Catholic and she goes to church at St. Mary's In Shelby, NC. Thomas Norkus is a Catholic also but he Is excommunicated because of his adulterous actions.

Dr. Fisher had to see a medical doctor because of the stress and posttraumatic stress syndrome that Dr. Fisher experienced because of this entire situation. Dr. Fisher is now on 2 blood pressure medications and a medication used for posttraumatic stress.

Dr. Fisher would have been willing to marry Thomas Norkus until she discovered him cheating on her. Dr. Fisher and Thomas did discuss marriage before they started dating. Dr. Fisher let Thomas Norkus know that she would not share a bed with him unless she married him. Thomas Norkus agreed to those terms.

Marriage is a contract between 2 people. Mrs. William interfered with a prospective marriage contract between Dr. Fisher and Thomas Norkus.

Negligent and Intentional infliction of emotional distress

Under negligence a duty of care is owed to all people who are foreseeable victims of a person's failure to take precautions. Mrs. Williams owed Dr. Fisher a duty of care by not having an affair with Dr. Fisher's boyfriend. The actual action of Mrs. Williams comes under the doctrine of Res ipsa loquitur (the thing speaks for itself). Dr. Fisher did suffer actual physical harm because of the stress of this situation. Dr. Fisher is now on 2 blood pressure medicines and a medicine used for posttraumatic stress.

Intentional infliction of emotional distress is intentional and extreme outrageous conduct that causes injury to the Plaintiff. Dr. Fisher had to see a medical doctor and start taking blood pressure medicine and medicine for post-traumatic stress. Mrs. Williams' adulterous conduct was intentional and extreme and caused physical injury to Dr. Fisher. Mrs. Williams recklessly disregarded the high probability that emotional distress will occur. This qualifies because of the Rest. 2d §46(1).

Case law concerning adultery and emotional distress

Cynthia Shackleford was awarded a $9 million lawsuit for Alienation of Affection against her husband's mistress in 2010. Carol Puryear was awarded $30,162,000 dollars in March 2011 in the case of Puryear v. Devin by Wake County judge Carl J. Fox. And that same year a Pitt County court awarded Dr Lynn Arcara $5.8 Million against Susan Pecoraro whom she said stole her husband away from her. Pecoraro had been the wife's closest friend prior to the illicit relationship with the husband. A Mecklenburg County jury awarded $1.4 million in May 2001 to former Davidson College wrestling coach, Thomas Oddo against Dr. Jeffrey Presser of West Palm Beach, Fla., after the coach's wife, Debra, left him for Presser (the jury verdict was later reduced by the NC Court of Appeals as excessive). A year 2000 verdict of $86,250 for alienation of affections and $15,000 for criminal conversation in the case of Pharr v. Beck, from Burke County was upheld on appeal. In 1997, in the case of Hutelmyer v. Cox, the Plaintiff wife was awarded $1 million against her husband's secretary who "dressed sexy at work" and had an affair with him destroying their marriage. In May 1991, in the case of Nunn v. Allen, a Richmond county jury awarded $100,000 in damages. I found this information on the Rice Law Blog. As I stated before Tom Norkus and Dr. Fisher were not married but Mrs. Williams is still married and the dysfunctional relationship which she has with her husband have interfered with Dr. Fisher's life. The adulterous relationship that Mrs. Williams had with Thomas Norkus destroyed Dr. Fisher's relationship with Thomas Norkus and is morally offensive to the community.

Dr. Fisher is praying to the court not to dismiss this case because of the civil, criminal, and moral issues involved. Dr. Fisher is praying to the court for a jury trial concerning the issues involved. Dr. Fisher is seeking compensatory damages and injunctions for the damage that occurred to her life as a result of Mrs. Emily Williams having an adulterous relationship with Thomas Norkus, the boyfriend of Dr. Fisher, in Dr. Fisher's home without Dr. Fisher's knowledge. The dysfunctional marriage between David Williams and his wife Emily Williams harmed Dr. Fisher's life and David Williams never denied the fact that he knew the adulterous relationship with Thomas Norkus was taking place between Thomas Norkus and his wife and by not denying he was admitting he knew. Which makes David Williams as guilty as his wife.

If David Williams did not know he can go after Thomas Norkus legally for Alienation of Affection or Criminal Conversation in the civil courts.

Dr. Fisher is praying to the court for David Williams and Mrs. Williams to compensate her for the difference which Thomas Norkus did not compensate Dr. Fisher for and Dr. Fisher can prove all amounts to the court.

Mrs. Williams is considered a principal in the first degree because Mrs. Williams conspired with Thomas Norkus to keep the adulterous affair between Thomas Norkus and Mrs. Williams so Thomas Norkus could continue to benefit financially because Dr. Fisher was living with Thomas Norkus. Dr. Fisher invested quite a bit of money into Thomas Norkus and their relationship. Including work on their home at 516 Northgate Ave, Charlotte, NC.

The punitive damages that Dr. Fisher is praying for from the court is 2 letters of apology from David Williams and his wife Emily Williams for their selfish acts that created havoc in Dr. Fisher's life. The letters of apology should be addressed to Dr. Fisher and can come thru their attorney. If it is proven that David Williams did not know anything, she does not expect an apology letter from him. Dr. Fisher will continue to pray that the Lord will repair the damage done to the marriage between David and Emily Williams caused by Emily Williams' adulterous relationship with Thomas Norkus. Dr. Fisher admits she still loves Thomas Norkus but she will never trust him again and she does not know when she will be able to forgive him. She keeps praying about everything. One of the reasons she brought this lawsuit is because Thomas Norkus committed felony fraud against Mutual Drug of NC, when he tried to open his own pharmacy. That is the main reason she involved the law also, because Thomas Norkus continually commits felony fraud. She is enclosing a copy of NCBOP issue in which he almost lost his pharmacy license because of felony fraud. As a pharmacist in the same profession she needed to let the legal authorities know about his criminal tendencies. Mr. and Mrs. Williams was not around when committed the fraud against Mutual Drug and neither was William Joe Goodman. I did not know about it until I started dating Thomas Norkus. Honestly, Thomas Norkus was able to get thru to me because I have a soft heart. When he told me about his trouble with the NCBOP, he began crying in my arms and begging me not to leave him. I stayed by his side until I discovered he was cheating on me.

Dr. Fisher is also praying to the court for any other compensation or punitive damages the court deems appropriate. Dr. Fisher plans to have the help of a licensed attorney at trial or in any settlement conference. However, Dr. Fisher does feel that the questions raised in her complaint should be decided by a jury. Dr. Fisher is requesting a jury trial in this matter.

Dr. Fisher admits that she is extremely upset because of this situation and suffered irreparable harm emotionally and mentally. Dr. Fisher was harmed financially and emotionally because of an adulterous relationship which occurred between Mrs. Williams and Thomas Norkus, Dr. Fisher's boyfriend at the time the adulterous relationship took place. Dr. Fisher was also morally and religiously offended by the conduct that took place in her own home. Fraud was committed against Dr. Fisher when the adulterous relationship started because Dr. Fisher was helping to pay for upgrades and repairs to the house and she was buying the groceries and cooking. Dr. Fisher also did the laundry of Thomas Norkus and had his house cleaned. Dr. Fisher would have left if she had known that Thomas Norkus was in an adulterous relationship (cheating on her) in what she considered her own house because of the money she invested in the house and in Thomas Norkus, her boyfriend. Dr. Fisher had let Thomas Norkus know that she would leave if he wanted to start dating other people. Dr. Fisher had no clue what was going on when she was not at home. Both Dr. Fisher and Thomas Norkus are pharmacists.

Dr. Fisher would like to apologize to the court for the emotion that is coming across to the court. And Dr. Fisher would like to apologize to the court for any mistakes she might make because she is still learning. Dr. Fisher does have an Executive Juris Doctor but is not a licensed attorney yet but she hopes to be licensed someday.

Dr. Fisher is also praying to the court to deny the motion of attorney fees that the attorney is requesting on behalf of Mr. and Mrs. Williams.

Because all legal questions stated in the complaint are either tort actions under civil and/or have criminal consequences or both, Dr. Fisher believes she does have verifiable legal issues under the North Carolina law and Federal Law.

Dr. Fisher is asking for injunctions in this lawsuit because of the irreparable harm suffered from the actions of Thomas Norkus, Mr. and Mrs. Williams, and William Joe Goodman. Mr. and Mrs. Williams should not be allowed to be in contact with Thomas Norkus or William Joe Goodman ever again because the contact between these people here resulted in fraud against Dr. Cynthia Fisher and extreme emotional and mental damage.

Dr. Fisher knows that David Williams can say he knew nothing about the adulterous relationship that took place between Thomas Norkus and his wife Emily Williams. If David Williams does deny knowledge of the affair, Dr. Fisher will believe him and voluntarily dismiss the complaint against him. I suggest he go after Thomas Norkus for any attorney fees he has had to pay because he is the one who had an adulterous relationship with his wife and caused all this.

The fact that Thomas Norkus and I were not married will be questioned. I was sharing his house and not his bed because of my religious beliefs. The issue is that Mrs. Emily Williams had an adulterous relationship with my boyfriend in my house. She is the one that is married but under North Carolina law both adulterers are equally guilty. The only reason I have an interest in her marriage is because she had an adulterous relationship with my boyfriend in my house. My relationship with Thomas Norkus is really none of her concern because I did not have an adulterous relationship with her husband.

Dr. Fisher thanks the court for its help in this matter.

Dr. Cynthia Ann Fisher
PharmD, EJD

CYNTHIA A. FISHER
PLAINTIFF,
Vs,
THOMAS NORKUS
DAVID WILLIAMS,
EMILY WILLIAMS,
WILLIAM JOE GOODMAN,
DEFENDANTS

DFENDANT AND WITNESS FIRST SET OF ADMISSIONS

TO: THOMAS NORKUS

NOW COMES THE PLAINTIFF, by and thru pro se, and pursuant to rule 36 of the North Carolina Rules of Civil Procedure and serves the following Requests for Admission upon the DEFEDANT AND WITNESS:

These Requests for Admissions are served upon you pursuant to Rule 36 of the Rules of Civil Procedure. You are reminded that pursuant to Rule 37 (c) of the Rules of Civil Procedure entitled "Expenses on Failure to Admit, "if you fail to admit to the genuineness of any document or the truth of the matter as requested under Rule 36, and if the Plaintiff thereafter proves the genuineness of the document or the truth of the matter, Plaintiff may apply to the Court for an order requiring you to pay reasonable expenses incurred in making that proof, including attorney's fees.

You are requested to admit for the purpose of this action only, within thirty (30) days of service hereof:

ADMISSIONS:

1. Lives at 516 Northgate Ave, Charlotte, NC.

   Admit_____ Deny_____

2. Adulterous relationships are immoral and a public nuisance.

   Admit_____ Deny_____

3. Adulterous relationships are a private nuisance.

   Admit_____ Deny_____

4. Adultery is a very selfish act because it hurts more than just one person.

   Admit_____ Deny_____

5. Cynthia Fisher spent in excess of $15,000 on him and his house in 2014.

   Admit_____ Deny_____

6. Thomas Norkus settled with Cynthia Fisher out of court for his part only.

Admit_____ Deny_____

7. Cynthia Fisher removed Thomas Norkus from her checking account as soon as she discovered he was cheating and no longer let him use her car.

   Admit_____ Deny_____

8. Thomas Norkus knew that Cynthia Fisher was religious and that she would leave him when she discovered that he was cheating on her.

   Admit_____ Deny_____

9. Cynthia Fisher did leave him after she discovered the cheating.

   Admit_____ Deny_____

10. Allowed Mrs. Williams to ride in Cynthia Fisher's car without her permission.

    Admit_____ Deny_____

11. Allowed Mrs. Williams access to food and other household items bought by Cynthia Fisher without Cynthia Fisher's permission.

    Admit_____ Deny_____

12. Knew that Cynthia Fisher was extremely sensitive about being lied to and used because of things that have occurred in her recent past.

    Admit_____ Deny_____

13. Told Cynthia Fisher that David Williams had an open relationship with his wife, Mrs. Emily Williams, when Cynthia Fisher discovered the cheating.

    Admit_____   Deny_____

14. Cynthia Fisher has accused him of lying concerning this issue.

    Admit_____   Deny_____

15. Thomas Norkus admitted to Cynthia Fisher that he was in an adulterous relationship when Cynthia Fisher confronted him after she caught them on the security cameras in their house.

    Admit_____   Deny_____

16. Thomas Norkus told Cynthia Fisher that she would not have caught him if she had not had the security cameras installed.

    Admit_____   Deny_____

17. Thomas Norkus agreed to have the security cameras installed.

    Admit_____   Deny_____

18. Thomas Norkus allowed William Joe Goodman to blackmail him for free rent because William Joe Goodman knew that Thomas Norkus was cheating on Cynthia Fisher.

    Admit_____   Deny_____

CYNTHIA A. FISHER
PLAINTIFF,
Vs,
THOMAS NORKUS
DAVID WILLIAMS,
EMILY WILLIAMS,
WILLIAM JOE GOODMAN,
DEFENDANTS

DEFENDANT (DAVID WILLIAMS) FIRST SET OF ADMISSIONS

Mathew R. Arnold
Attorney for David Williams
N.C. Bar No. : 31370
Arnold & Smith, PLLC
The Historic John Price Carr House
200 North McDowell Street
Charlotte, NC 28204
Telephone: 704-370-2828
Fax: 704-370-2202
Electronic Mail: mra@arnoldsmithlaw.com

NOW COMES THE PLAINTIFF, by and thru pro se, and pursuant to rule 36 of the North Carolina Rules of Civil Procedure and serves the following Requests for Admission upon the DEFEDANT AND WITNESS:

These Requests for Admissions are served upon you pursuant to Rule 36 of the Rules of Civil Procedure. You are reminded that pursuant to Rule 37 (c) of the Rules of Civil Procedure entitled "Expenses on Failure to Admit, "if you fail to admit to the genuineness of any document or the truth of the matter as requested under Rule 36, and if the Plaintiff thereafter proves the genuineness of the document or the truth of the matter, Plaintiff may apply to the Court for an order requiring you to pay reasonable expenses incurred in making that proof, including attorney's fees.

You are requested to admit for the purpose of this action only, within thirty (30) days of service hereof:

ADMISSIONS:

1. David Williams is the husband of Emily Williams

   Admit_____ Deny_____

2. David Williams knew about the adulterous affair between Thomas Norkus and his wife
   Emily Williams and did not care because he and his wife have an open marriage.

   Admit_____ Deny_____

3. David Williams is a Dean at Belmont Abbey College.

   Admit_____ Deny_____

4. David Williams is a Catholic.

   Admit_____ Deny_____

5. Belmont Abbey College is a Catholic College.

   Admit_____ Deny_____

6. Cynthia Fisher did let him (David Williams) know about the adulterous relationship between his wife (Emily Williams) and her boyfriend (Thomas Norkus) in an email.

Admit_____ Deny_____

7. Adultery is a public and private nuisance because it is immoral and a sin.

Admit_____ Deny_____

8. Adultery is immoral according to Catholics.

Admit_____ Deny_____

9. Adultery is a sin according to Catholics and the majority of the public.

Admit_____ Deny_____

10. Adultery is illegal according to NC law.

Admit_____ Deny_____

CYNTHIA A. FISHER
PLAINTIFF,
Vs,
THOMAS NORKUS
DAVID WILLIAMS,
EMILY WILLIAMS,
WILLIAM JOE GOODMAN,
DEFENDANTS

DEFENDANT (EMILY WILLIAMS) FIRST SET OF ADMISSIONS

Mathew R. Arnold
Attorney for Emily Williams
N.C. Bar No. : 31370
Arnold & Smith, PLLC
The Historic John Price Carr House
200 North McDowell Street
Charlotte, NC 28204
Telephone: 704-370-2828
Fax: 704-370-2202
Electronic Mail: mra@arnoldsmithlaw.com

NOW COMES THE PLAINTIFF, by and thru pro se, and pursuant to rule 36 of the North Carolina Rules of Civil Procedure and serves the following Requests for Admission upon the DEFEDANT AND WITNESS:

These Requests for Admissions are served upon you pursuant to Rule 36 of the Rules of Civil Procedure. You are reminded that pursuant to Rule 37 (c) of the Rules of Civil Procedure entitled "Expenses on Failure to Admit, "if you fail to admit to the genuineness of any document or the truth of the matter as requested under Rule 36, and if the Plaintiff thereafter proves the genuineness of the document or the truth of the matter, Plaintiff may apply to the Court for an order requiring you to pay reasonable expenses incurred in making that proof, including attorney's fees.

You are requested to admit for the purpose of this action only, within thirty (30) days of service hereof:

ADMISSIONS:

1. Emily Williams is the wife of David Williams.

   Admit_____ Deny_____

2. Emily Williams was only interested in Thomas Norkus for his money.

   Admit_____ Deny_____

3. Emily Williams works at Belmont Abbey College as an instructor

   Admit_____ Deny_____

4. Emily Williams is a Catholic.

   Admit____ Deny_____

5. Belmont Abbey College is a Catholic College.

   Admit____ Deny_____

6. Adultery is a public and private nuisance because it is immoral and a sin.

   Admit____ Deny_____

7. Adultery is immoral according to Catholics.

   Admit____ Deny_____

8. Adultery is a sin according to Catholics and the majority of the public.

   Admit____ Deny_____

9. Adultery is illegal according to NC law.

   Admit_____ Deny_____

10. Emily Williams never apologized to Cynthia Fisher for interfering and disrupting her life.

    Admit_____ Deny_____

11. Adultery is a selfish act and proves that the person or people committing adultery are selfish and only care about themselves.

    Admit_____ Deny_____

12. Adultery proves that you are putting your own selfish desires before God.

    Admit_____ Deny_____

13. Emily Williams did not have Cynthia Fisher's permission to ride in her car.

    Admit_____ Deny_____

14. Emily Williams did not have Cynthia Fisher's permission to have an adulterous relationship with her boyfriend Thomas Norkus.

    Admit_____ Deny_____

15. Emily Williams did not have Cynthia Fisher's permission to be in her house or use any household food or products that Cynthia Fisher bought.

    Admit_____ Deny_____

16. Cynthia Fisher left Thomas Norkus because she discovered the adulterous relationship (cheating) between Thomas Norkus and Emily Williams on the security cameras in the house.

   Admit_____   Deny_____

www.ingramcontent.com/pod-product-compliance
Lightning Source LLC
Chambersburg PA
CBHW051214170526
45166CB00005B/1889